Thomas Hood

Whims and Oddities

In Prose and Verse

Thomas Hood

Whims and Oddities
In Prose and Verse

ISBN/EAN: 9783337417659

Printed in Europe, USA, Canada, Australia, Japan

Cover: Foto ©Thomas Meinert / pixelio.de

More available books at **www.hansebooks.com**

FEBRUARY, 1860.

A LIST OF BOOKS

PUBLISHED BY

EDWARD MOXON & CO., DOVER STREET.

ILLUSTRATED EDITION OF TENNYSON'S PRINCESS.
WITH MACLISE'S ILLUSTRATIONS.

*In royal 8vo, cloth, price 16s., morocco 21s., illustrated with 26 Wood
Engravings by* THOMAS DALZIEL *and* GREEN,
from Designs by D. MACLISE, R.A.,

THE PRINCESS; A MEDLEY.
BY ALFRED TENNYSON, ESQ., D.C.L.,
POET LAUREATE.

Also, by the same Author,

TENNYSON'S POEMS.
TWELFTH EDITION. In one volume, foolscap 8vo, price 9s. cloth.

TENNYSON'S PRINCESS. A MEDLEY.
EIGHTH EDITION. Price 5s. cloth.

TENNYSON'S MAUD; AND OTHER POEMS.
THIRD EDITION. Price 5s. cloth.

TENNYSON'S IDYLLS OF THE KING.
Price 7s. cloth.

IN MEMORIAM. EIGHTH EDITION. Price 6s. cloth.

DYCE'S SHAKESPEARE.

In Six Vols., demy 8vo, price 4l. 4s.

THE

WORKS OF WILLIAM SHAKESPEARE.

THE TEXT REVISED BY THE REV. ALEXANDER DYCE.

" A minute examination has satisfied us that this is the best text
of Shakespeare which has yet been given to the world. * * * *
This at least is beyond doubt, that we have never possessed so admirable a text of Shakespeare before; and we would suggest to the
thousands of people who are always inquiring for something interesting to read, that they should read again the works of the monarch
of literature, and read him in the edition of Mr. Dyce."—QUARTERLY
REVIEW, January, 1859.

NEW AND ILLUSTRATED EDITION OF SHARPE'S EGYPT.

*In Two Vols., demy 8vo, price 24s. cloth, with upwards of 350 illus-
trations and Two Coloured Maps,*

THE HISTORY OF EGYPT,

FROM THE EARLIEST TIMES TO THE CONQUEST BY THE ARABS, A.D. 640.

BY SAMUEL SHARPE.

HAYDN'S DICTIONARY OF DATES.

In One Vol., demy 8vo, price 18s.

HAYDN'S DICTIONARY OF DATES.

Comprehending Remarkable Occurrences, Ancient and Modern—the
Foundation, Laws, and Governments of Countries—their Progress in
Civilisation, Industry, and Science—their Achievements in Arms—
their Civil, Military, and Religious Institutions—the Origin and
Advance of Human Arts and Inventions, with copious details relating to the British Empire. The whole comprehending a body of
Information, Classical, Political, and Domestic, from the earliest
accounts to the present time. NINTH EDITION, revised and greatly
enlarged by BENJAMIN VINCENT, Assistant Secretary and Keeper of
the Library of the Royal Institution of Great Britain.

In this Edition about Five Hundred new articles have been inserted;
a very great number of articles have been re-written; and in order
still more to adapt the work to educational purposes, numerous
biographical, geographical, literary, and scientific details have been
supplied.

" A volume containing upwards of 15,000 articles, and, perhaps,
more than 15 times 15,000 facts. What the London Directory is to the
merchant, this Dictionary of Dates will be found to be to those who are
searching after information, whether classical, political, domestic, or
general."—TIMES.

HALL'S FRAGMENTS.

A New Edition. In One Volume 8vo, price 10s. 6d. *cloth.*

CAPTAIN BASIL HALL'S

FRAGMENTS OF VOYAGES AND TRAVELS.

LAMB'S WORKS.

THE WORKS OF CHARLES LAMB.

In four volumes, foolscap 8vo, price 20s. cloth.

CONTENTS:

1. The Letters of Charles Lamb, with a Sketch of his Life. By Sir T. N. TALFOURD.—2. Final Memorials of Charles Lamb; consisting chiefly of his Letters not before published, with Sketches of some of his Companions. By Sir T. N. TALFOURD.—3. The Essays of Elia.— 4. Rosamund Gray, Recollections of Christ's Hospital, Poems, &c.

THE WORKS OF CHARLES LAMB.

In one volume 8vo, with Portrait and Vignette, price 16s. cloth.

THE ESSAYS OF ELIA.

In one volume, foolscap 8vo, price 6s. cloth.

WORKS BY THE LATE THOMAS HOOD.

HOOD'S POEMS. ELEVENTH EDITION.

In one volume, foolscap 8vo, price 7s. cloth.

HOOD'S POEMS OF WIT AND HUMOUR.

EIGHTH EDITION.   In one volume, foolscap 8vo, price 5s. cloth.

HOOD'S OWN ;

OR, LAUGHTER FROM YEAR TO YEAR.

A NEW EDITION. In one volume 8vo, illustrated by 350 Woodcuts, price 10s. 6d. cloth.

HOOD'S WHIMS AND ODDITIES,

IN PROSE AND VERSE.

With 87 Original Designs. A NEW EDITION. In one volume, foolscap 8vo, price 5s. cloth.

WORKS BY THE LATE S. T. COLERIDGE.
—◆—

COLERIDGE'S POEMS.

A New Edition. In one volume, foolscap 8vo, price 6s. cloth.

COLERIDGE'S DRAMATIC WORKS.

A New Edition. In one volume, foolscap 8vo, price 6s. cloth.

COLERIDGE'S AIDS TO REFLECTION.

Eighth Edition. In one volume, foolscap 8vo, price 6s. cloth.

COLERIDGE'S FRIEND.

A Series of Essays, to aid in the formation of Fixed Principles in Politics, Morals, and Religion, with Literary Amusements interspersed. Fourth Edition. In three volumes, foolscap 8vo, price 15s. cloth.

COLERIDGE'S ESSAYS ON HIS OWN TIMES.

In three volumes, foolscap 8vo, price 18s. cloth.

COLERIDGE ON THE CONSTITUTION OF CHURCH AND STATE.

Fourth Edition. In one volume, foolscap 8vo, price 5s. cloth.

COLERIDGE'S LAY SERMONS.

Third Edition. In one volume, foolscap 8vo, price 5s. cloth.

COLERIDGE'S CONFESSIONS OF AN INQUIRING SPIRIT.

Third Edition. In one volume, foolscap 8vo, price 4s. cloth.

COLERIDGE'S WORKS—*continued.*

COLERIDGE'S BIOGRAPHIA LITERARIA;

OR,

BIOGRAPHICAL SKETCHES OF MY LITERARY LIFE AND OPINIONS.

SECOND EDITION.   In two volumes, foolscap 8vo, price 18s. cloth.

COLERIDGE'S NOTES AND LECTURES UPON SHAKESPEARE,

AND SOME OF THE OLD POETS AND DRAMATISTS.

WITH OTHER LITERARY REMAINS.   In two volumes, foolscap 8vo, price 12s. cloth.

COLERIDGE'S NOTES ON ENGLISH DIVINES.

In two volumes, foolscap 8vo, price 12s. cloth.

COLERIDGE'S NOTES,

THEOLOGICAL, POLITICAL, AND MISCELLANEOUS.

In one volume, foolscap 8vo, price 6s. cloth.

ILLUSTRATED EDITIONS OF ROGERS'S POEMS.

ROGERS'S POEMS.

In one volume, illustrated by 72 Vignettes, from Designs by Turner and Stothard, price 16s. cloth.

ROGERS'S ITALY.

In one volume, illustrated by 56 Vignettes, from designs by Turner and Stothard, price 16s. cloth.

ROGERS'S POETICAL WORKS.

In one volume, foolscap 8vo, illustrated by numerous Woodcuts, price 9s. cloth.

WORKS BY THE LATE WILLIAM WORDSWORTH.

WORDSWORTH'S POETICAL WORKS.

In six volumes, fcap. 8vo, price 30s. cloth.

WORDSWORTH'S POETICAL WORKS.

In one volume, 8vo, with Portrait and Vignette, price 20s. cloth.

WORDSWORTH'S POETICAL WORKS.

In six pocket volumes, price 21s. cloth.

₊ *The above are the only* COMPLETE *Editions of Wordsworth's Poems.*

WORDSWORTH'S PRELUDE;

OR, GROWTH OF A POET'S MIND.

AN AUTOBIOGRAPHICAL POEM.

In one volume, foolscap 8vo, price 6s. cloth.

WORDSWORTH'S EXCURSION.

A POEM.

In one volume, foolscap 8vo, price 6s. cloth.

THE EARLIER POEMS OF WILLIAM WORDSWORTH.

In one volume, foolscap 8vo, price 6s. cloth.

SELECT PIECES FROM THE POEMS OF WILLIAM WORDSWORTH.

In one volume, illustrated by Woodcuts, price 6s. cloth, gilt edges.

KEATS'S POEMS.

✦

KEATS'S POETICAL WORKS.

In one volume, illustrated by 120 designs, Original and from the Antique, drawn on wood by GEORGE SCHARF, Jun., price 12s. cloth.

KEATS'S POETICAL WORKS.

In one volume, foolscap 8vo, price 5s. cloth.

SHELLEY'S WORKS.

— ✦ —

SHELLEY'S POEMS, ESSAYS, AND LETTERS
FROM ABROAD.

EDITED BY MRS. SHELLEY.

In one volume, medium 8vo, with Portrait and Vignette, price 12s. cloth.

SHELLEY'S POETICAL WORKS.

EDITED BY MRS. SHELLEY.

In three volumes, foolscap 8vo, price 15s. cloth.

SHELLEY'S ESSAYS, LETTERS FROM ABROAD.

TRANSLATIONS, AND FRAGMENTS.

EDITED BY MRS. SHELLEY.

In two volumes, foolscap 8vo, price 9s. cloth.

SHELLEY'S POETICAL WORKS.

In one volume, small 8vo, with Portrait and Vignette, price 7s. cloth.

DANA'S SEAMAN'S MANUAL; by the Author of "Two Years before the Mast." Containing: A Treatise on Practical Seamanship, with Plates; a Dictionary of Sea Terms; Customs and Usages of the Merchant Service; Laws relating to the Practical Duties of Master and Mariners. EIGHTH EDITION, revised and corrected in accordance with the most recent Acts of Parliament, by J. H. BROWN, Esq., Registrar-General of Merchant Seamen. Price 5s. cloth.

GOETHE'S FAUST. TRANSLATED INTO ENGLISH PROSE, with Notes. By A. HAYWARD, Esq., Q.C. SIXTH EDITION. Price 4s. cloth.

TALFOURD'S DRAMATIC WORKS. In one volume, foolscap 8vo, price 6s. cloth.

TAYLOR'S PHILIP VAN ARTEVELDE. In one volume, foolscap 8vo, price 3s. 6d. cloth.

TAYLOR'S EDWIN THE FAIR; ISAAC COMNENUS; THE EVE OF THE CONQUEST, and other Poems. In one volume, foolscap 8vo, price 3s. 6d. cloth.

HOGG'S LIFE OF SHELLEY. Post 8vo, Vols. I. and II., price 21s. cloth.

TRELAWNY'S RECOLLECTIONS OF THE LAST DAYS OF SHELLEY AND BYRON. Post 8vo, price 9s. cloth.

MILNES'S POEMS. In four volumes, foolscap 8vo, price 20s. cloth.

BRODERIP'S WAY-SIDE FANCIES. In one volume, foolscap 8vo, price 6s. cloth.

POETRY.—*Pocket Editions.*

WORDSWORTH'S POETICAL WORKS. In six volumes, price 21s. cloth.

WORDSWORTH'S EXCURSION. Price 3s. 6d. cloth.

ROGERS'S POETICAL WORKS. Price 5s. cloth.

CAMPBELL'S POETICAL WORKS. Price 3s. 6d. cloth.

KEATS'S POETICAL WORKS. Price 3s. 6d. cloth.

COLERIDGE'S POEMS. Price 3s. 6d. cloth.

SHELLEY'S MINOR POEMS. Price 3s. 6d. cloth.

PERCY'S RELIQUES OF ANCIENT ENGLISH POETRY. In three volumes, price 9s. cloth.

LAMB'S SPECIMENS OF ENGLISH DRAMATIC POETS. In two volumes, price 6s. cloth.

DODD'S BEAUTIES OF SHAKSPEARE. Price 3s. 6d. cloth.

BRADBURY AND EVANS, PRINTERS, WHITEFRIARS.

WHIMS AND ODDITIES.

FIRST AND SECOND SERIES.

WHIMS AND ODDITIES,

In Prose and Verse:

WITH EIGHTY-SEVEN ORIGINAL DESIGNS,

BY THOMAS HOOD.

"Why don't you get up behind?"

A NEW EDITION.

LONDON:

EDWARD MOXON & CO., DOVER STREET.

1860.

LONDON
BRADBURY AND EVANS, PRINTERS, WHITEFRIARS.

PREFACE.

WHEN I last made my best bow in this book, I imagined that the public, to use a nautical phrase, had "parted from their best bower;" but it was an agreeable mistake. The First and Second Series, being now, like Colman's "Two Single Gentlemen rolled into one," a request is made to me, to furnish the two-act piece with a new prologue. Possibly, as I have declared the near relationship of this work to the COMIC ANNUAL, the publisher wishes, by this unusual number of Prefaces, to connect it also with the Odes and *Addresses*. At all events, I accede to his humour, in spite of a reasonable fear that, at this rate, my Sayings will soon exceed my Doings.

To tell the truth, an Author does not much disrelish the call for these " more last words ; " and

I confess at once that I affix this preliminary postscript, with some pride and pleasure. A modern book, like a modern race-horse, is apt to be reckoned aged at six years old; and an Olympiad and half have nearly elapsed since the birth of my first editions. It is pleasant, therefore, to find, that what was done in black and white has not become quite grey in the interval;—to say nothing of the comfort, at such an advanced age, of still finding friends in public, as well as in private, to put up with one's Whims and Oddities.

Seriously, I feel very grateful for the kindness which has exhausted three impressions of this work, and now invites another. Come what may, this little book will now leave four imprints behind it,— and a horse could do no more.

T. HOOD.

WINCHMORE HILL,
January, 1832.

CONTENTS.

—◆—

FIRST SERIES.

WHIMS AND ODDITIES.

FIRST SERIES.

"O Cicero! Cicero! if to pun be a crime, 'tis a crime I have learned of thee: O Bias! Bias! if to pun be a crime, by thy example I was biassed."

SCRIBLERUS.

DEDICATION, TO THE REVIEWERS.

What is a modern Poet's fate?
To write his thoughts upon a slate ;—
The Critic spits on what is done,—
Gives it a wipe,—and all is gone. .

In presenting his Whims and Oddities to the Public, the Author desires to say a few words, which he hopes will not swell into a Memoir.

It happens to most persons, in occasional lively moments, to have their little chirping fancies and brain-crotchets, that skip out of the ordinary meadow-land of the mind. The Author has caught *his*, and clapped them up in paper and print, like grasshoppers in a cage. The judicious reader will look upon the trifling creatures accordingly, and not expect from them the flights of poetical winged horses.

At a future time, the Press may be troubled with some things of a more serious tone and purpose,—which the Author has resolved upon publishing, in despite of the advice of certain critical friends. His forte, they are pleased to say, is decidedly humourous:

but a gentleman cannot always be breathing his comic
vein.

It will be seen, from the illustrations of the present
work, that the Inventor is no artist;—in fact, he was
never "meant to draw"—any more than the tape-tied
curtains mentioned by Mr. Pope. Those who look at
his designs, with Ovid's Love of Art, will therefore be
disappointed;—his sketches are as rude and artless to
other sketches, as Ingram's rustic manufacture to the
polished chair. The designer is quite aware of their
defects: but when Raphael has bestowed seven odd
legs upon four Apostles, and Fuseli has stuck in a
great goggle head without an owner;—when Michael
Angelo has set on a foot the wrong way, and Hogarth
has painted in defiance of all the laws of nature and
perspective, he does hope that his own little enormi-
ties may be forgiven—that his sketches may look
interesting, like Lord Byron's Sleeper,—"with all
their errors."

Such as they are, the Author resigns his pen-and-
ink fancies to the public eye. He has more designs
in the wood; and if the present sample should be
relished, he will cut more, and come again, according
to the proverb, with a New Series.

ADDRESS

———◆———

THE first edition of Whims and Oddities being exhausted, I am called forward by an importunate publisher to make my best bow, and a new address to a discerning and indulgent public. Unaffectedly flattered by those who have bought this little work, and still more bound to those who have bound it, I adopt the usual attitude of a Thanksgiver, but with more than the usual sincerity. Though my head is in Cornhill, my hand is not on my Cheapside in making these professions. There is a lasting impression on my heart, though there is none on the shelves of the publisher.

To the Reviewers in general, my gratitude is eminently due for their very impartial friendliness. It would have sufficed to reconcile me to a far greater portion than I have met with, of critical viper-tuperation. The candid journalists, who have condescended to point out my little errors, deserve my particular

thanks. It is comely to submit to the hand of taste
and the arm of discrimination, and with the head
of deference I shall endeavour to amend (with one
exception) in a New Series.

I am informed that certain monthly, weekly, and
very every-day critics, have taken great offence at my
puns:—and I can conceive how some Gentlemen with
one idea must be perplexed by a double meaning.
To my own notion a pun is an accommodating word,
like a farmer's horse,—with a pillion for an extra
sense to ride behind;—it will carry single, however,
if required. The Dennises are merely a sect, and I
had no design to please, exclusively, those verbal
Unitarians.

Having made this brief explanation and acknow-
ledgment, I beg leave, like the ghost of the royal
Dane, to say "Farewell at once," and commend my
remembrance and my book together, to the kindness
of the courteous reader.

ADDRESS

TO THE THIRD EDITION.

—⧫—

It is not usual to have more than one grace before meat, one prologue before a play—one address before a work,—Cerberus and myself are perhaps the only persons who have had three prefaces. I thought, indeed, that I had said my last in the last impression, but a new Edition being called for, I came forward for a new exit, after the fashion of Mr. Romeo Coates —a Gentleman, notorious, like Autumn, for taking a great many leaves at his departure.

As a literary parent, I am highly gratified to find that the elder volume of Whims and Oddities does not get snubbed, as happens with a first child, at the birth of a second; but that the Old and New Series obtain fresh favour and friends for each other, and are likely to walk hand in hand like smiling brothers, towards posterity.

Whether a third volume will transpire is a secret still "warranted undrawn" even to myself;—there is,

I am aware, a kind of nonsense indispensable,—or sine qua non-sense—that always comes in welcomely to relieve the serious discussions of graver authors, and I flatter myself that my performances may be of this nature; but having parted with so many of my vagaries, I am doubtful whether the next November may not find me sobered down into a political economist.

WHIMS AND ODDITIES.

MORAL REFLECTIONS ON THE CROSS OF ST. PAUL'S.

THE man that pays his pence, and goes
   Up to thy lofty cross, St. Paul,
Looks over London's naked nose,
     Women and men :
     The world is all beneath his ken,
    He sits above the *Ball*.
He seems on Mount Olympus' top,
Among the Gods, by Jupiter! and lets drop
   His eyes from the empyreal clouds
     On mortal crowds.

Seen from these skies,
How small those emmets in our eyes!
   Some carry little sticks—and one
   His eggs—to warm them in the sun :

Dear! what a hustle,
And bustle!
And there's my aunt. I know her by her waist,
So long and thin,
And so pinch'd in,
Just in the pismire taste.

Oh! what are men?—Beings so small,
That, should I fall
Upon their little heads, I must
Crush them by hundreds into dust!

And what is life? and all its ages—
There's seven stages!
Turnham Green! Chelsea! Putney! Fulham!
Brentford! and Kew!
And Tooting, too!
And oh! what very little nags to pull 'em.
Yet each would seem a horse indeed,
If here at Paul's tip-top we'd got 'em;
Although, like Cinderella's breed,
They're mice at bottom.
Then let me not despise a horse,
Though he looks small from Paul's high cross!
Since he would be,—as near the sky,
—Fourteen hands high.

What is this world with London in its lap?
Mogg's Map.
The Thames, that ebbs and flows in its broad channel?
A *tidy* kennel.
The bridges stretching from its banks?
Stone planks.

Oh me! hence could I read an admonition
        To mad Ambition!
But that he would not listen to my call,
Though I should stand upon the cross, and *ball!*

VERY DEAF, INDEED.

THE PRAYSE OF IGNORANCE.

An Extract from an Oration delivered before the most grave and Learned Faculty of Padua, by the Admirable Crichton.

Now your Clowne knoweth none of the Boke-man's troubles, and his dayes be the longer; for he doth not vault upon the fierie Pegasus, but jumpes merrilye upon old Ball, who is a cart-horse, and singeth another man's song, which hath, it may be, thirty and six verses, and a burthen withal, and goes to a tune which no man knowes but himself. Alsoe, he wooes the ruddye Cicely, which is not a Muse, but as comely a maide of fleshe as needes be, and many daintye ballades are made of their loves, as may be read in our Poets, their Pastoralls; only that therein he is called Damon, which standes for Roger, and Cicely, belike, is ycleped Sylvia, as belongs to their pastorall abodes. Where they lead soe happye life as to stir up envye in the towne's women, who would faine become Shepherdesses, by hook and by crook, and get green gownes and lay down upon the sweet verdant grass. Oh, how pleasauntly they sit all the daye long under a shady tree, to hear the young lambes; but at night they listen to the plaintive Philomell, and the gallaunts doe make them chappe-lets: or, if it chance to be May, they goe a Mayinge, whilst the yonge buds smell sweetlye, and the littel birdes are whistlynge and hoppinge all about. Then Roger and Cicely sit adowne under the white

haw-thorne, and he makes love to her in a shepherd-
like waye, in the midst of her flocke. She doth not
minde sheepes'-eyes. Even like Cupid and Psyche,
as they are set forthe by a cunning Flemishe Limner,
as hath been my hap to behold in the Low Countrye,
wherein Cupid, with his one hand, is a toyinge with
the haires of his head; but with the other, he hand-
leth the fair neck of his mistresse, who sitteth
discreetlye upon a flowerie bank, and lookes down as
bescemes upon her shoon; for she is vain of her
modestye. This I have seen at the Hague.

And Roger sayth, O Cicely, Cicely, how prettye
you be; whereat she doth open her mouthe, and
smiles loudly; which, when he heares, he sayth again,
Nay, but I doe love thee passing well, and with that
lays a loud buss upon her cheek, which cannot blushe
by reason of its perfect ruddynesse. Anon, he
spreadeth in her lap the pink ribbands which he
bought at the wake, for her busking, and alsoe a great
cake of ginger brede, which causeth her heart to be in
her mouthe. Then, quoth he, The little Robins have
got their mates, and the prettye Finches be all paired,
and why sholde not we? And, quoth she, as he
kisseth her, O Robin, Robin, you be such a sweet-
billed bird, that I must needes crye "Aye." Wherefore, on the Sundaye, they go to the Parishe Churche,
that they may be joyned into one, and be no more
single. Whither they walk tenderlye upon their toes,
as if they stepped all the waye upon egges. And
Roger hath a brave bowpot at his bosom, which is full
of Heart's Ease; but Cicely is decked with ribbands,
a knot here, and a knot there, and her head is furnished after a daintye fashion, soe that she wishes,
belike, that she was Roger to see herselfe all round

about,—and content her eyes upon her own devices.
Whereas, Roger smells to his nosegaye; but his looks
travel, as the crabbe goeth, which is side-wayes,
towards Cicely; and he smiles sweetlye, to think how
that he is going to be made a husband-man, and alsoe
of the good cheere which there will be to eat that
daye. Soe he walks up to the altar with a stout
harte; and when the parson hath made an ende, he
kisseth Cicely afreshe, and their markes are regis-
tered as man and wife in the church bokes.

After which, some threescore yeares, it may befall
you to light on a grave-stone, and, on the wood
thereof, to read as followeth:—

"Here I bee, Roger Rackstrawe, which did live at
Dipmore Ende, of this Parishe—but now in this tomb.

> Time was that I did sowe and plough,
> That lyes beneathe the furrowes now;
> But though Death sowes me with his graine,
> I knowe that I shall spring againe."

Now is not this a life to be envyde, which needeth
so many men's paynes to paint its pleasures? For,
saving the Law clerkes, it is set forth by all that write
upon sheepe's skins, even the makers of pastoralls:
wherein your Clowne is constantly a figure of Poetry,
—being allwayes amongst the leaves. He is their
Jack-i'-the-Green.—Wherefore I crye, for my owne
part, Oh! that I were a Boore! Oh! that I were a
Boore! that troubleth no man, and is troubled of
none. Who is written, wherein he cannot reade,
and is mayde into Poetry, that yet is no Poet; for how
sholde he make songs, that knoweth not King Cad-
mus, his alphabet, to pricke them down withal?—

Seeing that he is nowayes learnede—nor hath never

bitten of the Apple of Knowledge, which was but a sowre crabbe apple, whereby Adam his wisdom-teeth were set on edge. Wherefore, he is much more a happye man, saying unto his lusty yonge Dame, We twaine be one fleshe.—But the Poet sayth to his mate, Thou art skin of my skin, and bone of my bone; soe that this saying is not a paradoxe,—That the Boke Man is a Dunce in being Wise,—and the Clowne is Wise, in being a Dunce.

MISS TREE.

A VALENTINE.

I.

On! cruel heart! ere these posthumous papers
  Have met thine eyes, I shall be out of breath;
Those cruel eyes, like two funereal tapers,
  Have only lighted me the way to death.
Perchance, thou wilt extinguish them in vapours,
  When I am gone, and green grass covereth
Thy lover, lost; but it will be in vain—
It will not bring the vital spark again.

II.

Ah! when those eyes, like tapers, burn'd so blue,
  It seemed an omen that we must expect
The sprites of lovers; and it boded true,
  For I am half a sprite—a ghost elect;
Wherefore I write to thee this last adieu,
  With my last pen—before that I effect
My exit from the stage; just stopp'd before
The tombstone steps that lead us to death's door.

III.

Full soon those living eyes, now liquid bright,
  Will turn dead dull, and wear no radiance, save
They shed a dreary and inhuman light,
  Illum'd within by glow-worms of the grave;

These ruddy cheeks, so pleasant to the sight,
  These lusty legs, and all the limbs I have,
Will keep Death's carnival, and, foul or fresh,
Must bid farewell, a long farewell, to flesh!

IV.

Yea, and this very heart, that dies for thee,
  As broken victuals to the worms will go;
And all the world will dine again but me—
  For I shall have no stomach;—and I know,
When I am ghostly, thou wilt sprightly be
  As now thou art: but will not tears of woe
Water thy spirits, with remorse adjunct,
When thou dost pause, and think of the defunct?

V.

And when thy soul is buried in a sleep,
  In midnight solitude, and little dreaming
Of such a spectre—what, if I should creep
  Within thy presence in such dismal seeming?
Thine eyes will stare themselves awake, and weep,
  And thou wilt cross thyself with treble screaming,
And pray with mingled penitence and dread
That I were less alive—or not so dead.

VI.

Then will thy heart confess thee, and reprove
  This wilful homicide which thou hast done:
And the sad epitaph of so much love
  Will eat into my heart, as if in stone:
And all the lovers that around thee move,
  Will read my fate, and tremble for their own;
And strike upon their heartless breasts, and sigh,
" Man, born of woman, must of woman die!"

C

VII.

Mine eyes grow dropsical—I can no more—
    And what is written thou may'st scorn to read,
Shutting thy tearless eyes.—'Tis done—'tis o'er—
    My hand is destin'd for another deed.
But one last word wrung from its aching core.
    And my lone heart in silentness will bleed;
Alas! it ought to take a life to tell
That one last word—that fare—fare—fare thee well!

"RICH AND RARE WERE THE GEMS SHE WORE."

"PLEASE TO RING THE BELLE."

— ✦ —

I.

I'LL tell you a story that's not in Tom Moore :—
Young Love likes to knock at a pretty girl's door :
So he call'd upon Lucy—'twas just ten o'clock—
Like a spruce single man, with a smart double knock.

II.

Now a hand-maid, whatever her fingers be at,
Will run like a puss when she hears a *rat*-tat :
So Lucy ran up—and in two seconds more
Had question'd the stranger and answer'd the door.

III.

The meeting was bliss ; but the parting was woe ;
For the moment will come when such comers must go:
So she kiss'd him, and whisper'd—poor innocent
    thing—
"The next time you come, love, pray come with a
    ring."

LOVE.

— ⚬ —

O Love! what art thou, Love? the ace of hearts,
   Trumping earth's kings and queens, and all its suits;
A player, masquerading many parts
   In life's odd carnival;—a boy that shoots,
From ladies' eyes, such mortal woundy darts;
   A gardener, pulling heart's-ease up by the roots;
The Puck of Passion—partly false—part real—
A marriageable maiden's " beau ideal."

O Love! what art thou, Love? a wicked thing,
   Making green misses spoil their work at school;
A melancholy man, cross-gartering?
   Grave ripe-fac'd wisdom made an April fool?
A youngster, tilting at a wedding ring?
   A sinner, sitting on a cuttie stool?
A Ferdinand de Something in a hovel,
Helping Matilda Rose to make a novel?

O Love! what art thou, Love? one that is bad
   With palpitations of the heart—like mine—
A poor bewilder'd maid, making so sad
   A necklace of her garters—fell design!
A poet, gone unreasonably mad,
   Ending his sonnets with a hempen line?
O Love!—but whither, now? forgive me, pray;
I'm not the first that Love hath led astray.

A RECIPE—FOR CIVILIZATION.

The following Poem—is from the pen of DOCTOR KITCHENER!—the most heterogeneous of authors, but at the same time—in the Sporting Latin of Mr. Egan,—a real Homo-*genius*, or a Genius of a Man! In the Poem, his CULINARY ENTHUSIASM, as usual——*boils over!* and makes it seem written, as he describes himself (see The Cook's Oracle)—with the Spit in one hand!—and the Frying Pan in the other,—while in the style of the rhymes it is Hudibrastic,——as if in the ingredients of Versification, he had been assisted by his BUTLER!

As a Head Cook, Optician—Physician, Music Master—Domestic Economist and Death-bed Attorney!—I have celebrated The Author elsewhere with approbation :—and cannot now place him upon the Table *as a Poet*,——without still being his LAUDER, a phrase which those persons whose course of classical reading recalls the INFAMOUS FORGERY on *the Immortal Bard of Eden!*——will find easy to understand.

SURELY, those sages err who teach
That man is known from brutes by speech,
Which hardly severs man from woman,
But not th' inhuman from the human,—
Or else might parrots claim affinity,
And dogs be doctors by latinity,—
Not t' insist, (as might be shown)
That beasts have gibberish of their own,
Which once was no dead tongue, tho' we
Since Esop's days have lost the key ;
Nor yet to hint dumb men,—and, still, not
Beasts that could gossip though they will not,
But play at dummy like the monkeys,
For fear mankind should make them flunkies.

Neither can man be known by feature
Or form, because so like a creature,
That some grave men could never shape
Which is the aped and which the ape,
Nor by his gait, nor by his height,
Nor yet because he's black or white,
But *rational*,—for so we call
The only COOKING ANIMAL!
The only one who brings his bit
Of dinner to the pot or spit,
For where's the lion e'er was hasty,
To put his ven'son in a pasty?
Ergo, by logic, we repute,
That he who cooks is not a brute,—
But Equus brutum est, which means,
If a horse had sense he'd boil his beans,
Nay, no one but a horse would forage
On naked oats instead of porridge,
Which proves, if brutes and Scotchmen vary,
The difference is culinary.
Further, as man is known by feeding
From brutes,—so men from men, in breeding,
Are still distinguished as they eat,
And raw in manners, raw in meat.—
Look at the polish'd nations hight,
The civilized—the most polite
Is that which bears the praise of nations
For dressing eggs two hundred fashions,
Whereas, at savage feeders look,—
The less refined the less they cook;
From Tartar grooms that merely straddle
Across a steak and warm their saddle,
Down to the Abyssinian squaw,
That bolts her chops and collops raw,

And, like a wild beast, cares as little
To dress her person as her victual,—
For gowns, and gloves, and caps, and tippets,
Are beauty's sauces, spice, and sippets,
And not by shamble bodies put on,
But those who roast and boil their mutton;
So Eve and Adam wore no dresses
Because they lived on water-cresses,
And till they learn'd to cook their crudities,
Went blind as beetles to their nudities.
For niceness comes from th' inner side
(As an ox is drest before his hide),
And when the entrail loathes vulgarity
The outward man will soon cull rarity,
For 'tis th' effect of what we eat
To make a man look like his meat,
As insects show their food's complexions :
Thus foplings' clothes are like confections.
But who, to feed a jaunty coxcomb,
Would have an Abyssian ox come ?—
Or serve a dish of fricassees,
To clodpoles in a coat of frize ?
Whereas a black would call for buffalo
Alive—and, no doubt, eat the offal too.
Now, (this premised) it follows then
That certain culinary men
Should first go forth with pans and spits
To bring the heathens to their wits,
(For all wise Scotchmen of our century
Know that first steps are alimentary ;
And, as we have prov'd, flesh pots and saucepans
Must pave the way for Wilberforce plans ;)
But Bunyan err'd to think the near gate
To take man's soul, was battering Ear gate,

When reason should have work'd her course
As men of war do—when their force
Can't take a town by open courage,
They steal an entry with its forage.
What reverend bishop, for example,
Could preach horn'd Apis from his temple ?
Whereas a cook would soon unseat him,
And make his own churchwardens eat him.
Not Irving could convert those vermin
Th' Anthropophages, by a sermon;
Whereas your Osborne,* in a trice,
Would " take a shin of beef and spice,"—
And raise them such a savoury smother,
No Negro would devour his brother,
But turn his stomach round as loth
As Persians, to the old black broth,—
For knowledge oftenest makes an entry,
As well as true love, thro' the pantry,
Where beaux that came at first for feeding
Grow gallant men and get good breeding ;—
Exempli gratia—in the West,
Ship-traders say there swims a nest
Lin'd with black natives, like a rookery,
But coarse as carrion crows at cookery.—
This race, though now call'd O. Y. E. men.
(To show they are more than A. B. C. men,)
Was once so ignorant of our knacks
They laid their mats upon their backs,
And grew their quartern loaves for luncheon
On trees that baked them in the sunshine.
As for their bodies, they were coated,
(For painted things are so denoted ;)

* Cook to the late Sir Joseph Banks.

But, the naked truth is, stark primevals,
That said their prayers to timber devils,
Allow'd polygamy—dwelt in wig-wams,—
And, when they meant a feast, ate big yams.—
And why ?—because their savage nook
Had ne'er been visited by Cook,—
And so they fared till our great chief
Brought them, not methodists, but beef,
In tubs,—and taught them how to live,
Knowing it was too soon to give,
Just then, a homily on their sins,
(For cooking ends ere grace begins)
Or hand his tracts to the untractable
Till they could keep a more exact table—
For nature has her proper courses,
And wild men must be back'd like horses,
Which, jockeys know, are never fit
For riding till they've had a bit
I' the mouth ; but then, with proper tackle,
You may trot them to a tabernacle ;
Ergo (I say) he first made changes
In the heathen modes, by kitchen ranges,
And taught the king's cook, by convincing
Process, that chewing was not mincing,
And in her black fist thrust a bundle
Of tracts abridg'd from Glasse and Rundell,
Where, ere she had read beyond Welsh rabbits,
She saw the spareness of her habits,
And round her loins put on a striped
Towel, where fingers might be wiped,
And then her breast clothed like her ribs,
(For aprons lead of course to bibs)
And, by the time she had got a meat-
Screen, veil'd her back, too, from the heat—

As for her gravies and her sauces,
(Tho' they reform'd the royal fauces,)
Her forcemeats and ragouts,—I praise not,
Because the legend further says not,
Except, she kept each Christian high-day,
And once upon a fat good Fry-day
Ran short of logs, and told the Pagan,
That turn'd the spit, to chop up Dagon!—

"THE COOK'S ORACLE."

ON THE POPULAR CUPID.

"TELL ME, MY HEART, CAN THIS BE LOVE."

THE figure above was copied, by permission, from a lady's Valentine. To the common apprehension, it represents only a miracle of stall-feeding—a babe-Lambert—a caravan-prodigy of grossness,—but, in the romantic mythology, it is the image of the Divinity of Love.—

In sober verity,—does such an incubus oppress the

female bosom? Can such a monster of obesity be
coeval with the gossamer natures of Sylph and Fairy
in the juvenile faith? Is this he—the buoyant
Camdeo,—that, in the mind's eye of the poetess,
drifts adown the Ganges in a lotus—

> " Pillow'd in a lotus flow'r
> Gather'd in a summer hour,
> Floats he o'er the mountain wave,
> Which would be a tall ship's grave ?"—

Is this personage the disproportionate partner for
whom Pastorella sigheth,—in the smallest of cots?—
Does the platonic Amanda (who is all soul) refer, in
her discourses on Love, to this palpable being, who is
all body ? Or does Belinda, indeed, believe that such
a substantial Sagittarius lies ambush'd in her perilous
blue eye ?

It is in the legend, that a girl of Provence was
smitten once, and died, by the marble Apollo: but
did impassioned damsel ever dote, and wither, beside
the pedestal of this preposterous effigy ? or, rather is
not the unseemly emblem accountable for the coyness
and proverbial reluctance of maidens to the approaches
of Love ?

I can believe in his dwelling alone in the heart—
seeing that he must occupy it to repletion ;—in his
constancy, because he looks sedentary and not apt to
roam. That he is given to melt—from his great
pinguitude. That he burneth with a flame, for so all
fat burneth—and hath languishings—like other bodies
of his tonnage. That he sighs—from his size.—

I dispute not his kneeling at ladies' feet—since it
is the posture of elephants,—nor his promise that the

homage shall remain eternal. I doubt not of his
dying,—being of a corpulent habit, and a short neck.
    Of his blindness—with that inflated pig's cheek.
But for his lodging in Belinda's blue eye, my whole
faith is heretic—*for she hath never a sty in it.*

"SON OF THE SLEEPLESS."

"THE LAST MAN."

'Twas in the year two thousand and one,
A pleasant morning of May,
I sat on the gallows-tree all alone,
A-chaunting a merry lay,—
To think how the pest had spared my life,
To sing with the larks that day!

When up the heath came a jolly knave,
Like a scarecrow, all in rags:
It made me crow to see his old duds
All abroad in the wind, like flags:—
So up he came to the timbers' foot
And pitch'd down his greasy bags.—

Good Lord! how blithe the old beggar was!
At pulling out his scraps,—
The very sight of his broken orts
Made a work in his wrinkled chaps:
"Come down," says he, "you Newgate-bird,
And have a taste of my snaps!"——

Then down the rope, like a tar from the mast,
I slided, and by him stood;
But I wished myself on the gallows again
When I smelt that beggar's food,
A foul beef-bone and a mouldy crust;
"Oh!" quoth he, "the heavens are good!"

Then after this grace he cast him down:
Says I, "You'll get sweeter air
A pace or two off, on the windward side,"
For the felons' bones lay there.
But he only laugh'd at the empty skulls,
And offered them part of his fare.

"I never harm'd *them*, and they won't harm me:
Let the proud and the rich be cravens!"
I did not like that strange beggar man,
He look'd so up at the heavens.
Anon he shook out his empty old poke;
"There's the crumbs," saith he, "for the ravens!"

It made me angry to see his face,
It had such a jesting look;
But while I made up my mind to speak,
A small case-bottle he took:
Quoth he, "though I gather the green water-cress
My drink is not of the brook!"

Full manners-like he tender'd the dram;
Oh, it came of a dainty cask!
But, whenever it came to his turn to pull,
"Your leave, good Sir, I must ask;
But I always wipe the brim with my sleeve,
When a hangman sups at my flask!"

And then he laugh'd so loudly and long,
The churl was quite out of breath;
I thought the very Old One was come
To mock me before my death,
And wish'd I had buried the dead men's bones
That were lying about the heath!

But the beggar gave me a jolly clap—
"Come, let us pledge each other,
For all the wide world is dead beside,
And we are brother and brother—
I've a yearning for thee in my heart,
As if we had come of one mother.

" I've a yearning for thee in my heart
That almost makes me weep,
For as I pass'd from town to town
The folks were all stone-asleep,—
But when I saw thee sitting aloft,
It made me both laugh and leap!"

Now a curse (I thought) be on his love,
And a curse upon his mirth,—
An' it were not for that beggar man
I'd be the King of the earth,—
But I promis'd myself an hour should come
To make him rue his birth—

So down we sat and bous'd again
Till the sun was in mid-sky,
When, just as the gentle west-wind came,
We hearken'd a dismal cry ;
" Up, up, on the tree," quoth the beggar man,
" Till these horrible dogs go by !"

And, lo ! from the forest's far-off skirts,
They came all yelling for gore,
A hundred hounds pursuing at once,
And a panting hart before,
Till he sunk adown at the gallows' foot
And there his haunches they tore !

His haunches they tore, without a horn
To tell when the chase was done ;
And there was not a single scarlet coat
To flaunt it in the sun !—
I turn'd, and look'd at the beggar man,
And his tears dropt one by one !

And with curses sore he chid at the hounds,
Till the last dropt out of sight,
Anon, saith he, " let's down again,
And ramble for our delight,
For the world's all free, and we may choose
A right cozie barn for to-night !"

D

With that, he set up his staff on end,
And it fell with the point due West;
So we far'd that way to a city great,
Where the folks had died of the pest—
It was fine to enter in house and hall,
Wherever it liked me best;

For the porters all were stiff and cold,
And could not lift their heads;
And when we came where their masters lay,
The rats leapt out of the beds;
The grandest palaces in the land
Were as free as workhouse sheds.

But the beggar man made a mumping face,
And knock'd at every gate:
It made me curse to hear how he whin'd,
So our fellowship turn'd to hate,
And I bade him walk the world by himself,
For I scorn'd so humble a mate!

So *he* turn'd right and *I* turn'd left,
As if we had never met;
And I chose a fair stone house for myself,
For the city was all to let;
And for three brave holydays drank my fill
Of the choicest that I could get.

And because my jerkin was coarse and worn,
I got me a properer vest;
It was purple velvet, stitch'd o'er with gold,
And a shining star at the breast!—
'Twas enough to fetch old Joan from her grave
To see me so purely drest!—

But Joan was dead and under the mould,
And every buxom lass;
In vain I watch'd, at the window pane,
For a Christian soul to pass!
But sheep and kine wander'd up the street,
And browz'd on the new-come grass.—

When lo! I spied the old beggar man,
And lustily he did sing!—
His rags were lapp'd in a scarlet cloak,
And a crown he had like a King;
So he stept right up before my gate
And danc'd me a saucy fling!

Heaven mend us all!—but, within my mind,
I had kill'd him then and there;
To see him lording so braggart-like
That was born to his beggar's fare;
And how he had stol'n the royal crown
His betters were meant to wear.

But God forbid that a thief should die
Without his share of the laws!
So I nimbly whipt my tackle out,
And soon tied up his claws,—
I was judge myself, and jury, and all,
And solemnly tried the cause.

But the beggar man would not plead, but cried
Like a babe without its corals,
For he knew how hard it is apt to go
When the law and a thief have quarrels,—
There was not a Christian soul alive
To speak a word for his morals.

D 2

Oh, how gaily I doff'd my costly gear,
And put on my work-day clothes;
I was tired of such a long Sunday life,—
And never was one of the sloths;
But the beggar man grumbled a weary deal,
And made many crooked mouths.

So I haul'd him off to the gallows' foot,
And blinded him in his bags;
'Twas a weary job to heave him up,
For a doom'd man always lags;
But by ten of the clock he was off his legs
In the wind, and airing his rags!

So there he hung, and there I stood,
The LAST MAN left alive,
To have my own will of all the earth:
Quoth I, now I shall thrive!
But when was ever honey made
With one bee in a hive!

My conscience began to gnaw my heart,
Before the day was done,
For other men's lives had all gone out,
Like candles in the sun!—
But it seem'd as if I had broke, at last,
A thousand necks in one!

So I went and cut his body down
To bury it decentlie;
God send there were any good soul alive
To do the like by me!
But the wild dogs came with terrible speed,
And bay'd me up the tree!

My sight was like a drunkard's sight,
And my head began to swim,
To see their jaws all white with foam,
Like the ravenous ocean brim ;—
But when the wild dogs trotted away
Their jaws were bloody and grim!

Their jaws were bloody and grim, good Lord!
But the beggar man, where was he ?—
There was nought of him but some ribbons of rags
Below the gallows' tree !—
I know the Devil, when I am dead,
Will send his hounds for me !—

I've buried my babies one by one,
And dug the deep hole for Joan,
And cover'd the faces of kith and kin,
And felt the old churchyard stone
Go cold to my heart, full many a time,
But I never felt so lone!

For the lion and Adam were company,
And the tiger him beguil'd ;
But the simple kine are foes to my life,
And the household brutes are wild.
If the veriest cur would lick my hand,
I could love it like a child !

And the beggar man's ghost besets my dream,
At night to make me madder,—
And my wretched conscience within my breast,
Is like a stinging adder ;—
I sigh when I pass the gallows' foot,
And look at the rope and ladder !—

For hanging looks sweet,—but alas! in vain
My desperate fancy begs,—
I must turn my cup of sorrows quite up,
And drink it to the dregs,—
For there is not another man alive,
In the world, to pull my legs!

"PIGMY AND CRANE."

BACKING THE FAVOURITE!

"O, MY BONNIE, BONNIE PET!"

On a pistol, or a knife!
For I'm weary of my life,—
   My cup has nothing sweet left to flavour it;
My estate is out at nurse,
And my heart is like my purse—
   And all through backing of the Favourite!

At dear O'Neil's first start,
I sported all my heart,—
   Oh, Becher, he never marr'd a braver hit!
For he cross'd her in her race,
And made her lose her place,
   And there was an end of that Favourite!

Anon, to mend my chance,
For the Goddess of the Dance *
  I pin'd, and told my enslaver it;
But she wedded in a canter,
And made me a Levanter,
  In foreign lands to sigh for the Favourite!

Then next Miss M. A. Tree
I adored, so sweetly she
  Could warble like a nightingale and quaver it;
But she left that course of life
To be Mr. Bradshaw's wife,
  And all the world lost on the Favourite!

But out of sorrow's surf
Soon I leap'd upon the turf,
  Where fortune loves to wanton it and waver it;
But standing on the pet,
"Oh my bonny, bonny Bet!"
  Black and yellow pull'd short up with the Favourite!

Thus flung by all the crack,
I resolv'd to cut the pack,—
  The second-raters seem'd then a safer hit!
So I laid my little odds
Against Memnon! Oh, ye Gods!
  Am I always to be floored by the Favourite!

---

  * The late favourite of the King's Theatre, who left the *pas seul* of life, for a perpetual *Ball*. Is not that her effigy now commonly borne about by the Italian image vendors—an ethereal form holding a wreath with both hands above her head—and her husband, in emblem, beneath her foot?

THE BALLAD OF

"SALLY BROWN, AND BEN THE CARPENTER."

— ✦ —

I HAVE never been vainer of any verses than of my
part in the following Ballad. Dr. Watts, amongst
evangelical nurses, has an enviable renown—and
Campbell's Ballads enjoy a snug genteel popularity.
"Sally Brown" has been favoured, perhaps, with as
wide a patronage as the Moral Songs, though its circle
may not have been of so select a class as the friends
of "Hohenlinden." But I do not desire to see it
amongst what are called Elegant Extracts. The
lamented Emery, drest as Tom Tug, sang it at his
last mortal Benefit at Covent Garden;—and, ever
since, it has been a great favourite with the watermen of Thames, who time their oars to it, as the
wherry-men of Venice time theirs to the lines of
Tasso. With the watermen, it went naturally to
Vauxhall :—and, over land, to Sadler's Wells. The
Guards, not the mail coach, but the Life Guards,—
picked it out from a fluttering hundred of others—all
going to one air—against the dead wall at Knights-
bridge. Cheap Printers of Shoe Lane, and Cowcross,
(all pirates!) disputed about the Copyright, and published their own editions,—and, in the meantime, the
Authors, to have made bread of their song, (it was

poor old Homer's hard ancient case!) must have sung it about the streets. Such is the lot of Literature! the profits of "Sally Brown" were divided by the Ballad Mongers:—it has cost, but has never brought me, a half-penny.

FAITHLESS SALLY BROWN.

AN OLD BALLAD.

I.

Young Ben he was a nice young man,
    A carpenter by trade;
And he fell in love with Sally Brown,
    That was a lady's maid.

II.

But as they fetch'd a walk one day,
    They met a press-gang crew;
And Sally she did faint away,
    While Ben he was brought to.

III.

The Boatswain swore with wicked words,
    Enough to shock a saint,
That though she did seem in a fit,
    'Twas nothing but a feint.

IV.

" Come, girl," said he, " hold up your head,
    He'll be as good as me;
For when your swain is in our boat,
    A boatswain he will be."

V.

So when they'd made their game of her,
    And taken off her elf,
She rous'd, and found she only was
    A coming to herself.

VI.

" And is he gone, and is he gone ?"
    She cried, and wept outright :
" Then I will to the water side,
    And see him out of sight."

VII.

A waterman came up to her,—
    " Now, young woman," said he,
" If you weep on so, you will make
    Eye-water in the sea."

VIII.

" Alas ! they've taken my beau Ben
    To sail with old Benbow ;"
And her woe began to run afresh,
    As if she'd said, Gee woe !

IX.

Says he, " they've only taken him
    To the Tender-ship, you see ;"
" The Tender-ship," cried Sally Brown,
    " What a hard-ship that must be !

X.

" Oh ! would I were a mermaid now,
    For then I'd follow him ;
But Oh !—I'm not a fish-woman,
    And so I cannot swim.

XI.

"Alas! I was not born beneath
    The virgin and the scales,
So I must curse my cruel stars,
    And walk about in Wales."

XII.

Now Ben had sail'd to many a place
    That's underneath the world;
But in two years the ship came home,
    And all her sails were furl'd.

XIII.

But when he call'd on Sally Brown,
    To see how she got on,
He found she'd got another Ben,
    Whose Christian-name was John.

XIV.

"O Sally Brown, O Sally Brown,
    How could you serve me so,
I've met with many a breeze before,
    But never such a blow!"

XV.

Then reading on his 'bacco box,
    He heav'd a bitter sigh,
And then began to eye his pipe,
    And then to pipe his eye.

XVI.

And then he tried to sing "All's Well,"
    But could not though he tried;
His head was turn'd, and so he chew'd
    His pigtail till he died.

XVII.

His death, which happen'd in his birth,
  At forty-odd befell :
They went and told the sexton, and
  The sexton toll'd the bell.

CHRISTMAS PANTOMIME.

A COMPLAINT AGAINST GREATNESS.

"O, THAT THIS TOO SOLID FLESH WOULD MELT!"

I AM an unfortunate creature, the most wretched of
all that groan under the burden of the flesh. I am
fainting, as they say of kings, under my oppressive
greatness. A miserable Atlas, I sink under the world
of—myself.

But the curious will here ask me for my name. I
am then, or they say I am, "The Reverend Mr. Farmer,
a four-years' old Durham Ox, fed by himself, upon oil
cake and mangel-wurzel:" but I resemble that worthy

agricultural Vicar only in my fat living. In plain
truth, I am an unhappy candidate for the show at
Sadler's, not "the Wells," but the Repository. They
tell me I am to bear the bell, (as if I had not enough
to bear already!) by my surpassing tonnage—and,
doubtless, the prize-emblem will be proportioned to
my uneasy merits. With a great Tom of Lincoln
about my neck—alas! what will it comfort me to have
been "commended by the judges."

Wearisome and painful was my Pilgrim-like progress
to this place, by short and tremulous steppings, like
the digit's march upon a dial. My owner, jealous of
my fat, procured a crippled drover, with a withered
limb, for my conductor; but even _he_ hurried me beyond
my breath. The drawling hearse left me labouring
behind; the ponderous fly-waggon passed me like a
bird upon the road, so tediously slow is my pace. It
just sufficeth, Oh, ye thrice happy Oysters! that have
no locomotive faculty at all, to distinguish that I am
not at rest. Wherever the grass grew by the way-
side, how it tempted my natural longings—the cool
brook flowed at my very foot, but this short thick neck
forbade me to eat or drink: nothing but my redundant
dewlap is likely ever to graze on the ground!

If stalls and troughs were not extant, I must perish.
Nature has given to the Elephant a long flexible tube,
or trunk, so that he can feed his mouth, as it were, by
his nose; but is man able to furnish me with such an
implement? Or would he not still withhold it, lest I
should prefer the green herb, my natural delicious
diet, and reject his rank, unsavoury condiments?
What beast, with free will, but would repair to the
sweet meadow for its pasture; and yet how grossly
is he labelled and libelled? Your bovine servant,—

in the catalogue, is a " Durham Ox, *fed by himself*, (as if he had any election,) upon oil-cake."

I wonder what rapacious Cook, with an eye to her insatiable grease-pot and kitchen perquisites, gave the hint of this system of stall-feeding! What unctuous Hull Merchant, or candle-loving Muscovite, made this grossness a desideratum? If mine were, indeed, like the fat of the tender sucking pig, that delicate gluten! there would be reason for its unbounded promotion ; but to see the prize steak, loaded with that rank yellow abomination, (the lamp-lighters know its relish,) might wean a man from carnivorous habits for ever. Verily, it is an abuse of the Christmas holly, the emblem of Old English and wholesome cheer, to plant it upon such blubber. A gentlemanly entrail must be driven to extreme straits, indeed, (Davis's Straits,) to feel any yearnings for such a meal; and yet I am told that an assembly of gentry, with all the celebrations of full bumpers and a blazing chimney-pot, have honoured the broiled slices of a prize bullock, a dishful of stringy fibres, an animal cabbage-net, and that rank even hath been satisfied with its rankness.

Will the honourable club, whose aim it is thus to make the beastly nature more beastly, consider of this matter? Will the humane, when they provide against the torments of cats and dogs, take no notice of our condition? Nature, to the whales, and creatures of their corpulence, has assigned the cool deeps ; but we have no such refuge in our meltings. At least, let the stall-feeder confine his system to the uncleanly swine which chews not the cud; for let the worthy members conceive on the palate of imagination, the abominable returns of the refuse-linseed in our after ruminations. Oh! let us not suffer in vain! It may seem

presumption in a brute, to question the human wisdom; but, truly, I can perceive no beneficial ends, worthy to be set off against our sufferings. There must be, methinks, a nearer way of augmenting the perquisites of the kitchen-wench and the fire-man,—of killing frogs,—than by exciting them, at the expense of us poor blown-up Oxen, to a mortal inflation.

"O! THERE'S NOTHING HALF SO SWEET IN LIFE."

THE MERMAID OF MARGATE.

"ALL'S WELL THAT ENDS WELL."

"Alas! what perils do inviron
That man who meddles with a siren!"

HUDIBRAS.

On Margate beach, where the sick one roams,
 And the sentimental reads;
Where the maiden flirts, and the widow comes—
 Like the ocean—to cast her weeds;—

Where urchins wander to pick up shells,
  And the Cit to spy at the ships,—
Like the water gala at Sadler's Wells,—
  And the Chandler for watery dips ;—

There's a maiden sits by the ocean brim,
  As lovely and fair as sin !
But woe, deep water and woe to him
  That she snareth like Peter Fin !

Her head is crown'd with pretty sea-wares,
  And her locks are golden and loose ;
And seek to her feet, like other folks' heirs,
  To stand, of course, in her shoes !

And, all day long, she combeth them well,
  With a sea-shark's prickly jaw ;
And her mouth is just like a rose-lipp'd shell,
  The fairest that man e'er saw !

And the Fishmonger, humble as love may be,
  Hath planted his seat by her side ;
" Good even, fair maid !   Is thy lover at sea,
  To make thee so watch the tide ?"

She turn'd about with her pearly brows,
  And clasp'd him by the hand :—
" Come, love, with me ; I've a bonny house
  On the golden Goodwin Sand."

And then she gave him a siren kiss,
  No honeycomb e'er was sweeter :
Poor wretch ! how little he dreamt for this
  That Peter should be salt-Peter !

And away with her prize to the wave she leapt,
   Not walking, as damsels do,
With toe and heel, as she ought to have stept,
   But she hopt like a Kangaroo!

One plunge, and then the victim was blind,
   Whilst they gallop'd across the tide;
At last, on the bank he waked in his mind,
   And the Beauty was by his side.

One half on the sand, and half in the sea,
   But his hair all began to stiffen;
For when he look'd where her feet should be,
   She had no more feet than Miss Biffen!

But a scaly tail, of a dolphin's growth,
   In the dabbling brine did soak:
At last she open'd her pearly mouth,
   Like an oyster, and thus she spoke :—

"You crimpt my father, who was a skate ;—
   And my sister you sold—a maid ;
So here remain for a fishlike fate,
   For lost you are, and betray'd!"

And away she went, with a seagull's scream,
   And a splash of her saucy tail;
In a moment he lost the silvery gleam
   That shone on her splendid mail!

The sun went down with a blood-red flame,
   And the sky grew cloudy and black,
And the tumbling billows like leap-frog came,
   Each over the other's back!

Ah, me! it had been a beautiful scene,
　　With the safe terra-firma round;
But the green water-hillocks all seem'd to him,
　　Like those in a church-yard ground;

And Christians love in the turf to lie,
　　Not in watery graves to be;
Nay, the very fishes will sooner die
　　On the land than in the sea.

And whilst he stood, the watery strife
　　Encroached on every hand,
And the ground decreas'd—his moments of life
　　Seem'd measur'd, like Time's, by sand;

And still the waters foam'd in, like ale,
　　In front, and on either flank,
He knew that Goodwin and Co. must fail,
　　There was such a run on the bank.

A little more, and a little more,
　　The surges came tumbling in;
He sang the evening hymn twice o'er,
　　And thought of every sin!

Each flounder and plaice lay cold at his heart,
　　As cold as his marble slab;
And he thought he felt, in every part,
　　The pincers of scalded crab.

The squealing lobsters that he had boil'd,
　　And the little potted shrimps,
All the horny prawns, he had ever spoil'd,
　　Gnaw'd into his soul, like imps!

And the billows were wandering to and fro,
  And the glorious sun was sunk,
And Day, getting black in the face, as tho'
  Of the night-shade she had drunk!

Had there been but a smuggler's cargo adrift,
  One tub, or keg, to be seen,
It might have given his spirits a lift
  Or an *anker* where *Hope* might lean!

But there was not a box or a beam afloat,
  To raft him from that sad place;
Not a skiff, not a yawl, or a mackarel boat,
  Nor a smack upon Neptune's face.

At last, his lingering hopes to buoy,
  He saw a sail and a mast,
And called "Ahoy!"—but it was not a hoy,
  And so the vessel went past.

And with saucy wing that flapp'd in his face,
  The wild bird about him flew,
With a shrilly scream, that twitted his case,
  "Why, thou art a sea-gull too!"

And lo! the tide was over his feet;
  Oh! his heart began to freeze,
And slowly to pulse:—in another beat
  The wave was up to his knees!

He was deafen'd amidst the mountain-tops,
  And the salt spray blinded his eyes,
And wash'd away the other salt-drops
  That grief had caused to arise:—

But just as his body was all afloat,
  And the surges above him broke,
He was saved from the hungry deep by a boat,
  Of Deal—(but builded of oak).

The skipper gave him a dram, as he lay,
  And chafed his shivering skin;
And the Angel return'd that was flying away
  With the spirit of Peter Fin!

"OH, BREATHE NOT HIS NAME!"

MY SON, SIR.

—•—

IT happened, the other evening, that, intending to call in L—— Street, I arrived a few minutes before Hyson; when W * * * * *, seated beside the urn, his eyes shaded by his hand,—was catechising his learned progeny, the Master Hopeful, as if for a tea-table degree. It was a whimsical contrast, between the fretful pouting visage of the urchin, having his gums rubbed so painfully, to bring forward his wisdom-tooth—and the parental visage, sage, solemn, and satisfied, and appealing ever and anon by a dramatic side look, to the circle of smirking auditors.

W * * * * * was fond of this kind of display, eternally stirring up the child for exhibition with his troublesome long pole,—besides lecturing him through the diurnal vacations so tediously, that the poor urchin was fain,—for the sake of a little play,—to get into school again.

I hate all forcing-frames for the young intellect,—and the *Locke* system, which after all is but a *Canal* system for raising the babe-mind to unnatural levels. I pity the poor child, that is learned in alpha beta, but ignorant of top and taw—and was never so maliciously gratified, as when, in spite of all his promptings and leading questions, I beheld W * * * * * reddening, even to the conscious tips of his tingling

ears, at the boy's untimely inaptitude. Why could
he not rest contented, when the poor imp had
answered him already, "What was a Roman Em-
peror?"—without requiring an interpretation of
the Logos?

"MY SON, SIR."

AS IT FELL UPON A DAY.

— ◆ —

I WONDER that W———, the Ami des Enfans, has never written a sonnet, or ballad, on a girl that had broken her pitcher. There are in the subject the poignant heart's anguish for sympathy and description;—and the brittleness of jars and joys, with the abrupt loss of the watery fruits—(the *pumpkins* as it were) of her labours, for a moral. In such childish accidents there is a world of woe;—the fall of earthenware is to babes, as, to elder contemplations, the Fall of Man.

I have often been tempted myself to indite a didactic ode to that urchin in Hogarth, with the ruined pie-dish. What a lusty agony is wringing him—so that all for pity he could die;—and then, there is the instantaneous falling-on of the Beggar Girl, to lick up the fragments—expressively hinting how universally want and hunger are abounding in this miserable world,—and ready gaping at every turn, for such windfalls and stray Godsends. But, hark!—what a shrill, feline cry startleth the wide Aldgate!

Oh! what's befallen Bessy Brown,
    She stands so squailing in the street;
She's let her pitcher tumble down,
    And all the water's at her feet!

The little school-boys stood about,
    And laughed to see her pumping, pumping;
Now with a curtsey to the spout,
    And then upon her tiptoes jumping.

Long time she waited for her neighbours,
    To have their turns:—but she must lose
The watery wages of her labours,—
    Except a little in her shoes!

Without a voice to tell her tale,
    And ugly transport in her face;
All like a jugless nightingale,
    She thinks of her bereaved case.

At last she sobs—she cries—she screams !—
    And pours her flood of sorrows out,
From eyes and mouth, in mingled streams,
    Just like the lion on the spout.

For well poor Bessy knows her mother
    Must lose her tea, for water's lack,
That Sukey burns—and baby-brother
    Must be dry-rubb'd with huck-a-back !

"POOR-TRAY CHARMANT."

A FAIRY TALE.

On Hounslow heath—and close beside the road,
  As western travellers may oft have seen,—
A little house some years ago there stood,
      A minikin abode;
And built like Mr. Birkbeck's, all of wood:
The walls of white, the window shutters green;—
Four wheels it had at North, South, East, and West,
      (Tho' now at rest)
On which it used to wander to and fro',
Because its master ne'er maintain'd a rider,
      Like those who trade in Paternoster Row;
But made his business travel for itself,
      Till he had made his pelf,
And then retired—if one may call it so,
      Of a roadsider.

Perchance, the very race and constant riot
Of stages, long and short, which thereby ran,
Made him more relish the repose and quiet
      Of his now sedentary caravan;
Perchance, he lov'd the ground because 'twas common,
      And so he might impale a strip of soil,
      That furnish'd, by his toil,
Some dusty greens, for him and his old woman;—
And five tall hollyhocks, in dingy flower:
Howbeit, the thoroughfare did no ways spoil

His peace, unless, in some unlucky hour,
A stray horse came and gobbled up his bow'r!

But tired of always looking at the coaches,
The same to come,—when they had seen them one day!
    And, used to brisker life, both man and wife
Began to suffer N U E's approaches,
And feel retirement like a long wet Sunday :—
So, having had some quarters of school breeding,
They turn'd themselves, like other folks, to reading;
But setting out where others nigh have done,
    And being ripen'd in the seventh stage,
      The childhood of old age,
Began, as other children have begun,—
Not with the pastorals of Mr. Pope,
    Or Bard of Hope,
Or Paley ethical, or learned Porson,—
But spelt, on Sabbaths, in St. Mark, or John,
And then relax'd themselves with Whittington,
    Or Valentine and Orson—
But chiefly fairy tales they loved to con,
And being easily melted in their dotage,
      Slobber'd,—and kept
      Reading,—and wept
Over the white Cat, in their wooden cottage.

    Thus reading on—the longer
They read, of course, their childish faith grew stronger
In Gnomes, and Hags, and Elves, and Giants grim,—
If talking Trees and Birds reveal'd to him,
She saw the flight of Fairyland's fly-waggons,
    And magic-fishes swim
In puddle ponds, and took old crows for dragons.—
Both were quite drunk from the enchanted flagons;

When, as it fell upon a summer's day,
    As the old man sat a feeding
       On the old babe-reading,
Beside his open street-and-parlour door,
    A hideous roar
Proclaim'd a drove of beasts was coming by the way.

Long-horn'd, and short, of many a different breed,
Tall, tawny brutes, from famous Lincoln-levels
      Or Durham feed;
With some of those unquiet black dwarf devils
      From nether side of Tweed,
      Or Firth of Forth;
Looking half wild with joy to leave the North,—
With dusty hides, all mobbing on together,—
When,—whether from a fly's malicious comment
Upon his tender flank, from which he shrank;
      Or whether
Only in some enthusiastic moment,—
However, one brown monster, in a frisk,
Giving his tail a perpendicular whisk,
Kick'd out a passage thro' the beastly rabble;
And after a pas seul,—or, if you will, a
Horn-pipe before the Basket-maker's villa,
      Leapt o'er the tiny pale,—
Back'd his beef-steaks against the wooden gable,
And thrust his brawny bell-rope of a tail
      Right o'er the page,
      Wherein the sage
Just then was spelling some romantic fable.

The old man, half a scholar, half a dunce,
Could not peruse,—who could?—two tales at once:
      And being huff'd

At what he knew was none of Riquet's Tuft,
          Bang'd-to the door,
But most unluckily enclosed a morsel
Of the intruding tail, and all the tassel :—
          The monster gave a roar,
And bolting off with speed, increased by pain,
The little house became a coach once more,
And, like Macheath, "took to the road" again!

Just then, by fortune's whimsical decree,
The ancient woman stooping with her crupper
Towards sweet home, or where sweet home should be,
Was getting up some household herbs for supper ;
Thoughtful of Cinderella, in the tale,
And quaintly wondering if magic shifts
Could o'er a common pumpkin so prevail,
To turn it to a coach ;—what pretty gifts
Might come of cabbages, and curly kale ;
Meanwhile she never heard her old man's wail,
Nor turn'd, till home had turn'd a corner, quite
          Gone out of sight!

At last, conceive her, rising from the ground,
Weary of sitting on her russet clothing :
          And looking round
          Where rest was to be found,
There was no house—no villa there—no nothing !
          No house !
          The change was quite amazing ;
It made her senses stagger for a minute,
The riddle's explication seem'd to harden ;
But soon her superannuated *nous*
Explained the horrid mystery ;—and raising
Her hand to heaven, with the cabbage in it,

On which she meant to sup,—
" Well! this *is* Fairy Work! I'll bet a farden,
Little Prince Silverwings has ketch'd me up,
And set me down in some one else's garden!"

MASTER GRAHAM.

THE SPOILED CHILD.

My Aunt Shakerly was of enormous bulk. I have not done justice to her hugeness in my sketch, for my timid pencil declined to hazard a sweep at her real dimensions. There is a vastness in the outline, of even moderate proportions, till the mass is rounded-off by shadows, that makes the hand hesitate, and apt to stint the figure of its proper breadth: how, then, should I have ventured to trace, like mapping in a Continent, the surpassing boundaries of my Aunt Shakerly!—

What a visage was hers!—the cheeks, a pair of hemispheres:—her neck literally swallowed up by a supplementary chin. Her arm, cased in a tight sleeve, was as the bolster,—her body like the feather bed of Ware. The waist, which, in other trunks, is an isthmus, was in hers only the middle zone of a continuous tract of flesh:—her ankles overlapped her shoes.

With such a figure, it may be supposed that her habits were sedentary.—When she did walk, the Tower Quay, for the sake of the fresh river-breeze, was her favourite resort. But never, in all her water-side promenades, was she hailed by the uplifted finger of the Waterman. With looks purposely averted he declined, tacitly, such a Fairlopian Fair.—The Hackney-coach driver, whilst she halted over against him, mustering up all her scanty puffings for an exclamation, drove off to the nether pavement, and pleaded a prior call. The chairman, in answer to her signals —had just broken his poles.—Thus, her goings were cramped within a narrow circle: many thoroughfares, besides, being strange to her and inaccessible, such as Thames Street, through the narrow pavements;—others, like the Hill of Holborn,—from their impracticable steepness. How she was finally to master a more serious ascension, (the sensible incumbrance of the flesh clinging to her even in her spiritual aspirations) was a matter of her serious despondency—a picture of Jacob's Ladder, by Sir F. Bourgeois, confirming her, that the celestial staircase was without a landing.

For a person of her elephantine proportions, my Aunt was of a kindly nature—for I confess a prejudice against such Giantesses. She was cheerful, and eminently charitable to the poor,—although she did

F 2

not condescend to a personal visitation of their very
limited abodes. If she had a fault, it was in her
conduct towards children—not spoiling them by often
repeated indulgences, and untimely severities, the
common practice of bad mothers:—it was by a shorter
course that the latent and hereditary virtues of the
infant Shakerly were blasted in the bud.—

Oh, my tender cousin **! (for thou wert yet unbap-
tised.)   Oh! would thou had'st been,—my little
babe-cousin,—of a savager mother born!—For then,
having thee comfortably swaddled, upon a backboard,
with a hole in it, she would have hung thee up, out of
harm's way, above the mantel-shelf, or behind the
kitchen door—whereas, thy parent was no savage, and
so, having her hands full of other matters, she laid
thee down, helpless, upon the parlour chair!—

In the mean time, the " Herald " came—Next to an
easy seat, my Aunt dearly loved a police newspaper;—
when she had once plunged into its columns, the most
vital question obtained from her only a random answer;
—the world and the roasting-jack stood equally still.
—So, without a second thought, she dropped herself
on the nursing chair.   One little smothered cry—my
cousin's last breath, found its way into the upper air,
—but the still small voice of the reporter engrossed
the maternal ear.

My aunt never skimmed a newspaper, according to
some people's practice. She was as solid a reader as
a sitter, and did not get up, therefore, till she had
gone through the " Herald " from end to end.   When
she did rise,—which was suddenly,—the earth quaked
—the windows rattled—the ewers plashed over—the
crockery fell from the shelf—and the cat and rats ran
out together, as they are said to do from a falling house.

"Heyday!" said my uncle, above stairs, as he staggered from the concussion—and, with the usual curiosity, he referred to his pocket-book for the Royal Birthday. But the almanack not accounting for the explosion, he ran down the stairs, at the heels of the housemaid, and there lay my Aunt, stretched on the parlour-floor, in a fit. At the very first glimpse, he explained the matter to his own satisfaction, in three words—

"Ah—the apoplexy!"

Now the housemaid had done her part to secure him against this error, by holding up the dead child; but as she turned the body *edge-ways*, he did not perceive it. When he did see it—but I must draw a curtain over the parental agony—

*   *   *   *

About an hour after the catastrophe, an inquisitive she-neighbour called in, and asked if we should not have the Coroner to sit on the body:—but my uncle replied, "There was no need."—"But in cases, Mr. Shakerly, where the death is not natural."—"My dear Madam," interrupted my uncle,—"it was a natural death enough."

THE FALL OF THE DEER.

[FROM AN OLD MS.]

—◆—

Now the loud Crye is up, and harke!
The barkye Trees give back the Bark;
The House Wife heares the merrie rout,
And runnes,—and lets the beere run out,
Leaving her Babes to weepe,—for why?
She likes to heare the Deer Dogges crye,
And see the wild Stag how he stretches
The naturall Buck-skin of his Breeches,
Running like one of Human kind
Dogged by fleet Bailiffes close behind—
As if he had not payde his Bill
For Ven'son, or was owing still
For his two Hornes, and soe did get
Over his Head and Ears in Debt;—
Wherefore he strives to paye his Waye
With his long Legges the while he maye:—
But he is chased, like Silver Dish,
As well as anye Hart may wish
Except that one whose Heart doth beat
So faste it hasteneth his feet;—
And runninge soe, he holdeth Death
Four Feet from him,—till his Breath
Faileth, and slacking Pace at last,
From runninge slow he standeth faste,

With hornie Bayonettes at baye,
To baying Dogges around, and they
Pushing him sore, he pusheth sore,
And goreth them that seeke his Gore,—
Whatever Dogge his Horne doth rive
Is dead—as sure as he's alive!
See that courageous Hart doth fight
With Fate, and calleth up his might,
And standeth stout that he maye fall
Bravelye, and be avenged of all,
Nor like a Craven yeeld his Breath
Under the Jawes of Dogges and Death!

"HOW HAPPY COULD I BE WITH EITHER!"

DECEMBER AND MAY.

"Crabbed Age and Youth cannot live together."

SHAKSPEARE.

—◆—

I.

SAID Nestor, to his pretty wife, quite sorrowful one
    day,
" Why, dearest, will you shed in pearls those lovely
    eyes away ?
You ought to be more fortified;" " Ah, brute, be
    quiet, do,
I know I'm not so fortyfied, nor fiftyfied, as you!

II.

Oh, men are vile deceivers all, as I have ever heard,
You'd die for me you swore, and I—I took you at
    your word.
I was a tradesman's widow then—a pretty change
    I've made ;
To live, and die the wife of one, a widower by trade!"

III.

" Come, come, my dear, these flighty airs declare, in
    sober truth,
You want as much in age, indeed, as I can want in
    youth ;

Besides, you said you liked old men, though now at
    me you huff."
"Why, yes," she said, "and so I do—but you're not
    old enough!"

IV.

"Come, come, my dear, let's make it up, and have a
    quiet hive;
I'll be the best of men,—I mean,—I'll be the best
    alive!
Your grieving so will kill me, for it cuts me to the
    core."—
"I thank ye, Sir, for telling me—for now I'll grieve
    the more!"

"TAKE, O TAKE THOSE LIPS AWAY!"

A WINTER NOSEGAY.

O, WITHER'D winter Blossoms,
Dowager-flowers,—the December vanity.
In antiquated visages and bosoms,—
What are ye plann'd for,
Unless to stand for
Emblems, and peevish morals of humanity?

There is my Quaker Aunt,
A Paper-Flower,—with a formal border
No breeze could e'er disorder,
Pouting at that old beau—the Winter Cherry,

A pucker'd berry;
And Box, like tough-liv'd annuitant,—
        Verdant alway—
From quarter-day even to quarter-day;
And poor old Honesty, as thin as want,
        Well named—God-wot;
Under the baptism of the water-pot,
The very apparition of a plant;
        And why,
Dost hold thy head so high,
        Old Winter-Daisy;—
Because thy virtue never was infirm,
        Howe'er thy stalk be crazy?
That never wanton fly, or blighted worm,
Made holes in thy most perfect indentation?
        'Tis likely that sour leaf,
        To garden thief,
Forcepp'd or wing'd, was never a temptation;—
Well,—still uphold thy wintry reputation;
Still shalt thou frown upon all lovers' trial:
And when, like Grecian maids, young maids of ours
        Converse with flow'rs,
Then thou shalt be the token of denial.

        Away! dull weeds,
Born without beneficial use or needs!
Fit only to deck out cold winding-sheets;
And then not for the milkmaid's funeral-bloom,
        Or fair Fidele's tomb——
        To tantalise,—vile cheats!
Some prodigal bee, with hope of after-sweets,
        Frigid, and rigid,
        As if ye never knew
        One drop of dew,

Or the warm sun resplendent;
Indifferent of culture and of care,
Giving no sweets back to the fostering air,
Churlishly independent—
I hate ye, of all breeds!
Yea, all that live so selfishly—to self,
And not by interchange of kindly deeds—
Hence!—from my shelf!

"ALL IN THE DOWNS."

EQUESTRIAN COURTSHIP.

I.

It was a young maiden went forth to ride,
And there was a wooer to pace by her side;
His horse was so little, and hers so high,
He thought his angel was up in the sky.

II.

His love was great tho' his wit was small;
He bade her ride easy—and that was all.
The very horses began to neigh,—
Because their betters had nought to say.

III.

They rode by elm, and they rode by oak,
They rode by a church-yard, and then he spoke:—
"My pretty maiden, if you'll agree
You shall always amble through life with me."

IV.

The damsel answer'd him never a word,
But kick'd the gray mare, and away she spurr'd.
The wooer still follow'd behind the jade,
And enjoy'd—like a wooer—the dust she made.

v.

They rode thro' moss, and they rode thro' moor,
The gallant behind and the lass before:—
At last they came to a miry place,
And there the sad wooer gave up the chase.

vi.

Quoth he, "If my nag were better to ride,
I'd follow her over the world so wide.
Oh, it is not my love that begins to fail,
But I've lost the last glimpse of the grey mare's tail!"

"MY NATURE IS SUBDUED TO WHAT IT WORKS IN."

"SHE IS FAR FROM THE LAND."

— ◆ —

It has been my fortune, or misfortune, sometimes to witness the distresses of females upon shipboard;—that is, in such fresh-victual passages as to Ramsgate —or to Leith. How they can contemplate or execute those longer voyages, beyond Good Hope's Cape,— even with the implied inducements of matrimony,—is one of my standard wonders. There is a natural shrinking—a cat-like antipathy,—to water, in the lady-constitution,—(as the false Argonaut well remembered when he shook off Ariadne)—that seems to forbid such sea-adventures. Betwixt a younger daughter, in Hampshire for example,—and a Judge's son of Calcutta, there is, apparently, a great gulf fixed :—

How have I felt, and shuddered, for a timid, shrinking, anxious female, full of tremblings as an aspen,—about to set her first foot upon the stage—but it can be nothing to a maiden's debût on the deck of an East Indiaman.

Handkerchiefs waving—not in welcome, but in farewell,—Crowded boxes,—not filled with living Beauty and Fashion—but departing luggage. Not the mere noisy Gods of the gallery to encounter,—but those, more boisterous, of the wind and wave. And then, all before her,—the great salt-water Pit !—

As I write this, the figure of Miss Oliver rises up before me,—just as she looked on her first introduction, by the Neptune, to the Ocean. It was her first voyage,—and she made sure would be her last. Her storms commenced at Gravesend,—her sea began much higher up. She had qualms at Blackwall. At the Nore, she came to the mountain-billows of her imagination ; for however the ocean may disappoint the expectation, from the land,—on ship-board, to the uninitiated, it hath all its terrors.—The sailor's capfull of wind was to her a North-wester. Every splash of a wave shocked her, as if each brought its torpedo. The loose cordage did not tremble and thrill more to the wind than her nerves. At every tack of the vessel,—on all-fours, for she would not trust to her own feet, and the outstretched hand of courtesy,—she scrambled up to the higher side. Her back ached with straining against the bulwark, to preserve her own, and the ship's, perpendicular :—her eyes glanced right, left, above, beneath, before, behind—with all the alacrity of alarm. She had not organs enough of sight, or hearing, to keep watch against all her imagined perils; her ignorance of nautical matters, in the meantime, causing her to mistake the real sea-dangers for subjects of self-congratulation. It delighted her to understand that there were barely three fathoms of water between the vessel and the ground; —her notion had been, that the whole sea was bottomless.—When the ship struck upon a sand, and was left there high and dry by the tide, her pleasure was, of course, complete. "We could walk about," she said, "and pick up shells." I believe, she would have been as well contented, if our Neptune had been pedestalled upon a rock;—deep water and sea-room were the only subjects of her dread. When the vessel, therefore, got afloat again, the old terrors of the landswoman returned upon her with the former force. All possible marine difficulties and disasters were huddled, like an auction medley, in one lot, into her apprehension:

Cables entangling her,
Shipspars for mangling her,
Ropes, sure of strangling her;
Blocks over-dangling her;
Tiller to batter her,
Topmast to shatter her,
Tobacco to spatter her;
Boreas blustering,
Boatswain quite flustering,
Thunder clouds mustering
To blast her with sulphur—
If the deep don't engulph her;
Sometimes fear's scrutiny
Pries out a mutiny,

G

Sniffs conflagration,
Or hints at starvation :—
All the sea-dangers
Buccaneers, rangers,
Pirates, and Sallee-men,
Algerine galleymen,
Tornadoes and typhons,
And horrible syphons,
And submarine travels
Thro' roaring sea-navels ;
Every thing wrong enough,
Long-boat not long enough,
Vessel not strong enough ;
Pitch marring frippery,
The deck very slippery,
And the cabin—built sloping,
The Captain a-toping,
And the Mate a blasphemer,
That names his Redeemer,—
With inward uneasiness ;
The cook, known by greasiness,
The victuals beslubber'd,
Her bed—in a cupboard ;
Things of strange christening,
Snatch'd in her listening,
Blue lights and red lights
And mention of dead lights,
And shrouds made a theme of,
Things horrid to dream of,—
And *buoys* in the water
To fear all exhort her ;
Her friend no Leander,
Herself no sea gander,
And ne'er a cork jacket

On board of the packet ;
The breeze still a stiffening,
The trumpet quite deafening ;
Thoughts of repentance,
And doomsday and sentence ;
Every thing sinister,
Not a church minister,—
Pilot a blunderer,
Coral reefs under her,
Ready to sunder her ;
Trunks tipsy-topsy,
The ship in a dropsy ;
Waves oversurging her,
Syrens a-dirgeing her ;
Sharks all expecting her,
Sword-fish dissecting her,
Crabs with their hand-vices
Punishing land vices ;
Sea-dogs and unicorns,
Things with no puny horns,
Mermen carnivorous—
" Good Lord deliver us !"

The rest of the voyage was occupied,—excepting
one bright interval,—with the sea malady and sea-
horrors. We were off Flamborough Head. A heavy
swell, the consequence of some recent storm to the
Eastward, was rolling right before the wind upon the
land :—and, once under the shadow of the bluff pro-
montory, we should lose all the advantage of a saving
Westerly breeze. Even the seamen looked anxious :
but the passengers (save one) were in despair. They
were, already, bones of contention, in their own
misgivings, to the myriads of cormorants and water-

fowl inhabiting that stupendous cliff. Miss Oliver
alone was sanguine :—she was all nods, and becks, and
wreathed smiles ;—her cheeriness increased in proportion with our dreariness. Even the dismal pitching
of the vessel could not disturb her unseasonable levity ;
—it was like a lightening before death—but, at length,
the mystery was explained. She had springs of comfort that we knew not of. Not brandy,—for that we
shared in common ;—nor supplications,—for those we
had all applied to ;—but her ears, being jealously vigilant of whatever passed between the mariners, she had
overheard from the captain,—and it had all the sound,
to her, of a comfortable promise,—that " if the wind
held, we should certainly *go on shore.*"

" COME O'ER THE SEA."

FANCIES ON A TEA-CUP.

I LOVE to pore upon old china—and to speculate, from the images, on Cathay. I can fancy that the Chinese manners betray themselves, like the drunkard's, in their cups.—

How quaintly pranked and patterned is their vessel! —exquisitely outlandish, yet not barbarian.—How daintily transparent!—It should be no vulgar earth, that produces that superlative ware, nor does it so seem in the enamell'd landscape.

There, are beautiful birds; there—rich flowers and gorgeous butterflies, and a delicate clime, if we may credit the porcelain. There be also horrible monsters, dragons, with us obsolete, and reckoned fabulous; the main breed, doubtless, having followed Fohi (our Noah), in his wanderings thither from the Mount Ararat.—But how does that impeach the loveliness of Cathay?—There are such creatures even in Fairyland.

I long often to loiter in those romantic Paradises— studded with pretty temples—holiday pleasure grounds —the true Tea-Gardens. I like those meandering waters, and the abounding little islands.

And here is a Chinese nurse-maid,—Ho-Fi, chiding a fretful little Pekin child. The urchin hath just such another toy, at the end of a string, as might be purchased at our own Mr. Dunnett's. It argues an advanced state of civilization, where the children have many playthings; and the Chinese infants—witness their flying fishes and whirligigs, sold by the stray natives about our streets—are far-gone in such juvenile luxuries.

But here is a better token.—The Chinese are a polite people : for they do not make household, much less husbandry, drudges of their wives. You may read the women's fortune in their tea-cups. In nine cases out of ten, the female is busy only in the lady-like toils of the toilette. Lo! here, how sedulously the blooming Hy-son is pencilling the mortal arches, and curving the cross-bows of her eye-brows. A musical instrument, her secondary engagement, is at her almost invisible feet. Are such little extremities likely to be tasked with laborious offices?—Marry, in kicking, they must be ludicrously impotent,—but then she hath a formidable growth of nails.

By her side, the obsequious Hum is pouring his soft flatteries into her ear. When she walketh abroad, (here it is on another sample) he shadeth her at two miles off with his umbrella. It is like an allegory of Love triumphing over space. The lady is walking upon one of those frequent petty islets, on a plain, as if of porcelain, without any herbage, only a solitary flower springs up, seemingly by enchantment, at her fairy-like foot. The watery space between the lovers is aptly left as a blank, excepting her adorable shadow, which is tending towards her slave.

How reverentially is yon urchin presenting his flowers to the Grey-beard! So honourably is age considered in China! There would be some sense, *there*, in birth-day celebrations.

Here, in another compartment, is a solitary scholar,

apparently studying the elaborate didactics of Con-
Fuse-Ye.

The Chinese have, verily, the advantage of us upon
earthenware! They trace themselves as lovers, con-
templatists, philosophers :—whereas, to judge from
our jugs and mugs, we are nothing but sheepish piping
shepherds and fox-hunters.

PÈRE LA CHAISE.

THE STAG-EYED LADY.

A MOORISH TALE.

Scheherazade immediately began the following story.

—◆—

ALI Ben Ali (did you never read
  His wond'rous acts that chronicles relate,—
How there was one in pity might exceed
  The sack of Troy?) Magnificent he sate
Upon the throne of greatness—great indeed,
  For those that he had under him were great—
The horse he rode on, shod with silver nails,
Was a Bashaw—Bashaws have horses' tails.

Ali was cruel—a most cruel one!
  'Tis rumour'd he had strangled his own mother—
Howbeit such deeds of darkness he had done,
  'Tis thought he would have slain his elder brother
And sister too—but happily that none
  Did live within *harm's* length of one another,
Else he had sent the Sun in all its blaze
To endless night, and shorten'd the Moon's days.

Despotic power, that mars a weak man's wit,
  And makes a bad man—absolutely bad,
Made Ali wicked—to a fault :—'tis fit
  Monarchs should have some check-strings; but he had

No curb upon his will—no not a *bit*—
 Wherefore he did not reign well—and full glad
His slaves had been to hang him—but they falter'd,
And let him live unhang'd—and still unalter'd,

Until he got a sage-bush of a beard,
 Wherein an Attic owl might roost—a trail
Of bristly hair—that, honour'd and unshear'd,
 Grew downward like old women and cow's tail:
Being a sign of age—some grey appear'd,
 Mingling with duskier brown its warnings pale;
But yet not so poetic as when Time
Comes like Jack Frost, and whitens it in rime.

Ben Ali took the hint, and much did vex
 His royal bosom that he had no son,
No living child of the more noble sex,
 To stand in his Morocco shoes—not one
To make a negro-pollard—or tread necks
 When he was gone—doom'd, when his days were done.
To leave the very city of his fame
Without an Ali to keep up his name.

Therefore he chose a lady for his love,
 Singling from out the herd one stag-eyed dear;
So call'd, because her lustrous eyes, above
 All eyes, were dark, and timorous, and clear;
Then, through his Muftis piously he strove,
 And drumm'd with proxy-prayers Mohammed's ear,
Knowing a boy for certain must come of it,
Or else he was not praying to his *Profit.*

Beer will grow *mothery*, and ladies fair
   Will grow like beer; so did that stag-eyed dame:
Ben Ali, hoping for a son and heir,
   Boy'd up his hopes, and even chose a name
Of mighty hero that his child should bear;
   He made so certain ere his chicken came:
But oh! all worldly wit is little worth,
Nor knoweth what to-morrow will bring forth.

To-morrow came, and with to-morrow's sun
   A little daughter to this world of sins;—
Miss-fortunes never come alone—so one
   Brought on another, like a pair of twins:
Twins! female twins!—it was enough to stun
   Their little wits and scare them from their skins
To hear their father stamp, and curse and swear,
Pulling his beard because he had no heir.

Then strove their stag-eyed mother to calm down
   This his paternal rage, and thus addrest:
" O! Most Serene! why dost thou stamp and frown,
   And box the compass of the royal chest?
Ah! thou wilt mar that portly trunk, I own
   I love to gaze on!—Pr'ythee, thou hadst best
Pocket thy fists. Nay, love, if you so thin
Your beard, you'll want a wig upon your chin!"

But not her words, nor e'en her tears, could slack
   The quicklime of his rage, that hotter grew:
He called his slaves to bring an ample sack
   Wherein a woman might be *poked*—a few

Dark grimly men felt pity and look'd black
   At this sad order; but their slaveships knew
When any dared demur, his sword so bending
Cut off the " head and front of their offending."

For Ali had a sword, much like himself,
   A crooked blade, guilty of human gore—
The trophies it had lopp'd from many an elf
   Were stuck at his *head*-quarters by the score—
Nor yet in peace he laid it on the shelf,
   But jested with it, and his wit cut sore;
So that (as they of Public Houses speak)
He often did his dozen *butts* a week.

Therefore his slaves, with most obedient fears,
   Came with the sack the lady to enclose;
In vain from her stag-eyes " the big round tears
   Coursed one another down her innocent nose ;"
In vain her tongue wept sorrow in their ears;
   Though there were some felt willing to oppose,
Yet when their heads came in their heads, that minute,
Though 'twas a piteous *case*, they put her in it.

And when the sack was tied, some two or three
   Of these black undertakers slowly brought her
To a kind of Moorish Serpentine ; for she
   Was doom'd to have *a winding sheet of water*.
Then farewell, earth—farewell to the green tree—
   Farewell, the sun—the moon—each little daughter !
She's shot from off the shoulders of a black,
Like a bag of Wall's-End from a coalman's back.

The waters oped, and the wide sack full-fill'd
  All that the waters oped, as down it fell ;
Then closed the wave, and then the surface rill'd
  A ring above her, like a water-knell ;
A moment more, and all its face was still'd,
  And not a guilty heave was left to tell
That underneath its calm and blue transparence
A dame lay drowned in her sack, like Clarence.

But Heaven beheld, and awful witness bore,
  The moon in black eclipse deceased that night,
Like Desdemona smother'd by the Moor—
  The lady's natal star with pale affright
Fainted and fell—and what were stars before,
  Turn'd comets as the tale was brought to light ;
And all look'd downward on the fatal wave,
And made their own reflections on her grave.

Next night, a head—a little lady head,
  Push'd through the waters a most glassy face,
With weedy tresses, thrown apart and spread,
  Comb'd by 'live ivory, to show the space
Of a pale forehead, and two eyes that shed
  A soft blue mist, breathing a bloomy grace
Over their sleepy lids—and so she rais'd
Her *aqualine* nose above the stream, and gazed.

She oped her lips—lips of a gentle blush,
  So pale it seem'd near drowned to a white,—
She oped her lips, and forth there sprang a gush
  Of music bubbling through the surface light ;

The leaves are motionless, the breezes hush
   To listen to the air—and through the night
There come these words of a most plaintive ditty,
Sobbing as they would break all hearts with pity :

THE WATER PERI'S SONG.

Farewell, farewell, to my mother's own daughter,
   The child that she wet-nursed is lapp'd in the wave ;
The *Mussul*-man coming to fish in this water,
   Adds a tear to the flood that weeps over her grave.

This sack is her coffin, this water's her bier,
   This greyish *bath* cloak is her funeral pall ;
And, stranger, O stranger ! this song that you hear
   Is her epitaph, elegy, dirges, and all !

Farewell, farewell, to the child of Al Hassan,
   My mother's own daughter—the last of her race—
She's a corpse, the poor body ! and lies in this basin,
   And sleeps in the water that washes her face.

WALTON REDIVIVUS.

A NEW-RIVER ECLOGUE.

— ✦ —

> "My old New River hath presented no extraordinary novelties lately.
> But there Hope sits, day after day, speculating on traditionary gudgeons.
> I think she hath taken the Fisheries. I now know the reasons why our
> forefathers were denominated East and West Angles. Yet is there no
> lack of spawn, for I wash my hands in fishlets that come through the
> pump, every morning, thick as motelings—little things that perish un-
> timely, and never taste the brook."—*From a Letter of C. Lamb.*

[Piscator is fishing,—near the Sir Hugh Middleton's Head, without
either basket or cann. Viator cometh up to him, with an angling-rod and
a bottle.]

Via. GOOD morrow, Master Piscator. Is there any
sport afloat ?

Pis. I have not been here time enough to answer
for it. It is barely two hours agone since I put in.

Via. The fishes are shyer in this stream than in
any water that I know.

Pis. I have fished here a whole Whitsuntide through
without a nibble. But then the weather was not so
excellent as to-day. This nice shower will set the
gudgeons all agape.

Via. I am impatient to begin.

Pis. Do you fish with gut ?

Via. No—I bait with gentles.

Pis. It is a good taking bait: though my question

referred to the nature of your line.   Let me see your
tackle.   Why this is no line, but a ship's cable.   It is
a six-twist.   There is nothing in this water but you
may pull out with a single hair.

Via. What, are there no dace, nor perch ?—

Pis. I doubt not but there have been such fish here,
in former ages.   But now-a-days there is nothing of
that size.   They are gone extinct, like the mammoths.

Via. There was always such a fishing at 'em.   Where
there was one Angler in former times, there is now a
hundred.

Pis. A murrain on 'em !—A New-River fish, now-a-
days, cannot take his common swimming exercise
without hitching on a hook.

Via. It is the natural course of things, for man's
populousness to terminate other breeds.   As the
proverb says, "The more Scotchmen, the fewer her-
rings."   It is curious to consider the family of whales
growing thinner according to the propagation of parish
lamps.

Pis. Ay, and withal, how the race of man, who is
a terrestrial animal, should have been in the greatest
jeopardy of extinction by the element of water ;
whereas the whales, living in the ocean, are most liable
to be burnt out.

Via. It is a pleasant speculation.   But how is this ?
—I thought to have brought my gentles comfortably
in an old snuff-box, and they are all stark dead !

Pis. The odour hath killed them.   There is nothing
more mortal than tobacco, to all kinds of vermin.
Wherefore, a new box will be indispensable, though,
for my own practice I prefer my waistcoat pockets for
their carriage.   Pray mark this :—and in the meantime I will lend you some worms.

Via. I am much beholden : and when you come to Long Acre, I will faithfully repay you. But, look you, my tackle is still amiss. My float will not swim.

Pis. It is no miracle—for here is at least a good ounce of swan-shots upon your line. It is over-charged with lead.

Via. I confess, I am only used to killing sparrows, and such small fowls, out of the back-casement. But my ignorance shall make me the more thankful for your help and instruction.

Pis. There. The fault is amended. And now, observe,—you must watch your cork very narrowly, without even an eye-wink another way;—for, otherwise, you may overlook the only nibble throughout the day.

Via. I have a bite already !—my float is going up and down like a ship at sea.

Pis. No. It is only that house-maid dipping in her bucket, which causes the agitation you perceive. 'Tis a shame so to interrupt the honest Angler's diversion. It would be but a judgment of God, now, if the jade should fall in !

Via. But I would have her only drowned for some brief twenty minutes or so—and then restored again by the Surgeons. And yet I have doubts of the lawfulness of that dragging of souls back again, that have taken their formal leaves. In my conscience, it seems like flying against the laws of predestination.

Pis. It is a doubtful point;—for, on the other hand, I have heard of some that were revived into life by the Doctors, and came afterwards to be hanged.

Via. Marry ! 'tis pity such knaves' lungs were ever puff'd up again! It was good tobacco-smoke ill wasted!

Oh, how pleasant, now, is the angling, which furnishes us with matter for such agreeable discourse! Surely, it is well called a contemplative recreation, for I never had half so many thoughts in my head before!

Pis. I am glad you relish it so well.

Via. I will take a summer lodging hereabouts, to be near the stream. How pleasant is this solitude! There are but fourteen a-fishing here,—and of those but few men.

Pis. And we shall be still more lonely on the other side of the City Road.—Come, let's across. Nay, we'll put in our lines lower down. There was a butcher's wife dragged for, at this bridge, in the last week.

Via. Have you, indeed, any qualms of that kind?

Pis. No—but, hereabouts, 'tis likely the gudgeons will be gorged. Now, we are far enough. Yonder is the row of Colebrooke. What a balmy wholesome gust is blowing over to us from the cow-lair.

Via. For my part, I smell nothing but dead kittens —for here lies a whole brood in soak. Would you believe it,—to my phantasy, the nine days' blindness of these creatures smacks somewhat of a type of the human pre-existence. Methinks, I have had myself such a mysterious being, before I beheld the light. My dreams hint at it. A sort of world before eyesight.

Pis. I have some dim sympathy with your meaning. At the Creation, there was such a kind of blind-man's-buff work. The atoms jostled together, before there was a revealing sun. But are we not fishing too deep?

Via. I am afeard on't! Would we had a plummet! We shall catch weeds.

Pis. It would be well to fish thus at the bottom, if
we were fishing for flounders in the sea. But there,
you must have forty fathom, or so, of stout line; and
then, with your fish at the end, it will be the boy's old
pastime carried into another element. I assure you,
'tis like swimming a kite!

Via. It should be pretty sport—but hush! My
cork has just made a bob. It is diving under the
water!—Holla!—I have catch'd a fish!

Pis. Is it a great one?

Via. Purely, a huge one! Shall I put it into the
bottle?

Pis. It will be well,—and let there be a good
measure of water, too, lest he scorch against the glass.

Via. How slippery and shining it is!—Ah, he is
gone!

Pis. You are not used to the handling of a New-
River fish;—and, indeed, very few be. But hath he
altogether escaped?

Via. No; I have his chin here, which I was obliged
to tear off, to get away my hook.

Pis. Well, let him go:—it would be labour wasted
to seek for him amongst this rank herbage. 'Tis the
commonest of Anglers' crosses.

Via. I am comforted to consider he did not fall
into the water again, as he was without a mouth,—and
might have pined for years. Do you think there is
any cruelty in our Art?

Pis. As for other methods of taking fish, I cannot
say: but I think none in the hooking of them.—For,
to look at the gills of a fish, with those manifold red
leaves, like a housewife's needle-book, they are
admirably adapted to our purpose; and manifestly
intended by Nature to stick our steel in.

Via. I am glad to have the question so comfortably resolved,—for, in truth, I have had some misgivings. —Now, look how dark the water grows! There is another shower towards.

Pis. Let it come down, and welcome. I have only my working-day clothes on. Sunday coats spoil holidays. Let every thing hang loose, and time too will sit easy.

Via. I like your philosophy. In this world, we are the fools of restraint. We starch our ruffs till they cut us under the ear.

Pis. How pleasant it would be to discuss these sentiments over a tankard of ale !—I have a simple bashfulness against going into a public tavern, but I think we could dodge into the Castle, without being much seen.

Via. And I have a sort of shuddering about me, that is willing to go more frankly in. Let us put up, then.—By my halidom! here is a little dead fish hanging at my hook :—and yet I never felt him bite.

Pis. 'Tis only a little week-old gudgeon, and he had not strength enough to stir the cork. However, we may say boldly, that we have caught a fish.

Via. Nay, I have another here, in my bottle. He was sleeping on his back at the top of the water, and I got him out nimbly with the hollow of my hand.

Pis. We have caught a brace then ;—besides the great one that was lost amongst the grass. I am glad on't, for we can bestow them upon some poor hungry person in our way home. It is passable good sport for the place.

Via. I am satisfied it must be called so. But the next time I come hither, I shall bring a reel with me, and a ready-made minnow, for I am certain there

must be some marvellous huge pikes here; they
always make a scarcity of other fish. However, I
have been bravely entertained, and, at the first holiday, I will come to it again.

PISCATOR.

"LOVE ME, LOVE MY DOG,"

SEEMS, at first sight, an unreasonable demand. May I profess no tenderness for Belinda without vowing an attachment to Shock? Must I feel an equal warmth towards my bosom friend and his greyhound? Some country gentlemen keep a pack of dogs. Am I expected to divide my personal regard for my Lord D. amongst all his celebrated fox-hounds?

I may be constitutionally averse to the whole canine species; I have been bitten, perhaps, in my

infancy by a mastiff, or pinned by a bull-dog. There
are harrowing tales on record of hydrophobia, of
human barkings, and inhuman smotherings. A dog
may be my bugbear. Again, there are differences in
taste. One man may like to have his hand licked all
over by a grateful spaniel; but I would not have my
extremity served so—even by the human tongue.

But the proverb, so arrogant and absolute in
spirit, becomes harmless in its common application.
The terms are seldom enforced, except by persons
that a gentleman is not likely to embrace in his affection—rat-catchers, butchers and bull-baiters, tinkers
and blind mendicants, beldames and witches. A
slaughterman's tulip-eared puppy, is as liable to
engage one's liking as his chuckle-headed master.
When a courtier makes friends with a drover, he will
not be likely to object to a sheep-dog as a third party
in the alliance.

" Love me," says Mother Sawyer, "love my dog."

Who careth to dote on either a witch or her familiar? The proverb thus loses half of its oppression :
in other cases, it may become a pleasant fiction, an
agreeable confession. I forget what pretty Countess it
was, who made confession of her tenderness for a
certain sea-captain, by her abundant caresses of his
Esquimaux wolf-dog. The shame of the avowal became milder, (as the virulence of the small-pox is
abated, after passing through the constitution of a
cow,) by its transmission through the animal.

In like manner, a formal young Quaker and Qua-
keress—perfect strangers to each other, and who
might otherwise have sat mum-chance together for
many hours—fell suddenly to romping, merely through

the maiden's playfulness with Obadiah's terrier. The dog broke the ice of formality,—and, as a third party, took off the painful awkwardness of self-introduction.

Sir Ulic Mackilligut, when he wished to break handsomely with Mistress Tabitha Bramble, kicked her cur. The dog broke the force of the affront, and the knight's gallantry was spared the reproach of a direct confession of disgust towards the spinster; as the lady took the aversion to herself only as the brute's ally.

My step-mother Hubbard, and myself, were not on visiting terms for many years. Not, we flattered ourselves, through any hatred or uncharitableness, disgraceful between relations, but from a constitutional antipathy on the one side, and a doting affection on the other—to a dog. My breach of duty and decent respect was softened down into my dread of hydrophobia :—my second-hand parent even persuaded herself, that I was jealous of her regard for Bijou. It was a comfortable self-delusion on both sides,—but the scape-goat died, and then, having no reasonable reason to excuse my visits, we came to an open rupture. There was no hope of another favourite.—My step-mother had no general affection for the race, but only for that particular cur. It was one of those incongruous attachments, not accountable to reason, but seemingly predestined by fate. The dog was no keepsake—no favourite of a dear deceased friend ;—ugly as the brute was, she loved him for his own sake,—not for any fondness and fidelity, for he was the most ungrateful dog, under kindness, that I ever knew;—not for his vigilance, for he was never wakeful. He was not useful, like a turnspit ; nor accomplished, for he could not dance. He had not personal beauty even,

to make him a welcome object; and yet, if my rela-
tion had been requested to display her jewels, she
would have pointed to the dog, and have answered, in
the very spirit of Cornelia,—"There is my Bijou."

Conceive, Reader, under this endearing title, a
hideous dwarf-mongrel, half pug and half terrier, with
a face like a frog's—his goggle-eyes squeezing out of
his head :—a body like a barrel-churn, on four short
bandy legs,—as if, in his puppyhood, he had been ill-
nursed—terminating in a tail like a rabbit's. There
is only one sound in nature, similar to his barking :—
to hear his voice, you would have looked, not for a dog,
but for a duck. He was fat, and scant of breath. It
might have been said, that he was stuffed alive ;—but
his loving mistress, in mournful anticipation of his
death, kept a handsome glass case, to hold his mummy.
She intended, like Queen Constance, to " stuff out his
vacant garment with his form ;"—to have him ever
before her, " in his habit as he lived ;"—but that hope
was never realised.

In those days there were dog-stealers, as well as
slave-dealers,—the kidnapping of the canine, as of the
Negro-victim, being attributable to his skin.

One evening, Bijou disappeared. A fruitless search
was made for him at all his accustomed haunts,—but
at day-break the next morning,—stripped naked of his
skin,—with a mock paper frill,—and the stump of a
tobacco-pipe stuck in his nether jaw,—he was discovered, set upright against a post !

My step-mother's grief was ungovernable. Tears,
which she had not wasted on her deceased step-
children, were shed then. In her first transport, a
reward of £100 was offered for the apprehension of
the murderers, but in vain.

The remains of Bijou, such as they were, she caused to be deposited under the lawn.

I forget what popular poet was gratified with ten guineas for writing his epitaph; but it was in the measure of the " Pleasures of Hope."

"O LIST UNTO MY TALE OF WOE!"

REMONSTRATORY ODE,

FROM THE ELEPHANT AT EXETER CHANGE, TO MR. MATHEWS,
AT THE ENGLISH OPERA-HOUSE.

" —— See with what courteous action,
He beckons you to a more removed ground."—*Hamlet*.

[WRITTEN BY A FRIEND.]

Oh, Mr. Mathews! Sir!
(If a plain elephant may speak his mind,
And that I have a mind to speak I find
          By my inward stir)
I long have thought, and wished to say, that we
Mar our well-merited prosperity
          By being such near neighbours.
My keeper now hath lent me pen and ink,
Shov'd in my truss of lunch, and tub of drink,
          And left me to my labours.
The whole menagerie is in repose,
The Coatamundi is in his Sunday clothes,
Watching the Lynx's most unnatural doze;
The Panther is asleep, and the Macaw;
The Lion is engaged on something raw;
          The white Bear cools his chin
          'Gainst the wet tin;
And the confined old Monkey's in the straw:
All the nine little Lionets are lying
Slumbering in milk, and sighing;
          Miss Cross is sipping ox-tail soup,
          In her front coop,

So here's the happy mid-day moment;—yes,
I seize it, Mr Mathews, to address
     A word or two
       To you
On the subject of the ruin which must come
By both being in the Strand, and both at home
  On the same nights; two treats
     So very near each other,
      As, oh my brother!
To play old gooseberry with both receipts.

     When you begin
Your summer fun, three times a week, at eight,
   And carriages roll up, and cits roll in,
 I feel a change in Exeter 'Change's change.
And, dash my trunk! I hate
To ring my bell, when you ring yours, and go
With a diminish'd glory through *my* show!
    It is most strange;
But crowds that meant to see me eat a stack,
And sip a water-butt or so, and crack
   A root of mangel-wurzel with my foot,
    Eat little children's fruit,
    Pick from the floor small coins,
And then turn slowly round and show my India-rubber
    loins:
  'Tis strange—most strange, but true,
  That these same crowds seek *you!*
  Pass *my* abode, and pay at *your* next door!
    It makes me roar
  With anguish when I think of this; I go
  With sad severity my nightly rounds
    Before one poor front row,
    My fatal funny foe!

And when I stoop, as duty bids, I sigh
And feel that, while poor elephantine I,
   Pick up a sixpence, you pick up the pounds!

      Could you not go?
Could you not take the Cobourg or the Surrey?
Or Sadler's Wells,—(I am not in a hurry,
I never am!) for the next season?—oh!
      Woe! woe! woe!
To both of us, if we remain; for not
In silence will I bear my altered lot,
To have you merry, sir, at my expense;
      No man of any sense,
No true great person (and we both are great
In our own ways) would tempt another's fate.
      I would myself depart
      In Mr. Cross's cart;
But, like Othello, "am not easily moved."
There's a nice house in Tottenham Court, they say,
Fit for a single gentleman's small play;
      And more conveniently near your home;
      You'll easily go and come.
Or get a room in the City—in some street—
Coachmaker's Hall, or the Paul's Head,
      Cateaton Street;
Any large place, in short, in which to get your bread;
      But do not stay, and get
      Me into the Gazette!

      Ah! The Gazette!
I press my forehead with my trunk, and wet
My tender cheek with elephantine tears,
      Shed of a walnut size
      From my wise eyes,

To think of ruin after prosperous years.
            What a dread case would be
            For me—large me!
To meet at Basinghall Street, the first and seventh
            And the eleventh!
        To undergo (D————n!)
            My last examination!
        To cringe, and to surrender,
        Like a criminal offender,
All my effects—my bell-pull, and my bell,
My bolt, my stock of hay, my new deal cell.
            To *post* my ivory, Sir!
And have some curious commissioner
Very irreverently search my trunk;
            'Sdeath! I should die
With rage, to find a tiger in possession
    Of my abode; up to his yellow knees
In my old straw; and my profound profession
    Entrusted to two beasts of assignees!

The truth is simply this,—if you *will* stay
            Under my very nose,
            Filling your rows
Just at my feeding time, to see *your* play,
            My mind's made up,
            No more at nine I sup,
Except on Tuesdays, Wednesdays, Fridays, Sundays,
            From eight to eleven,
            As I hope for heaven,
On Thursdays, and on Saturdays, and Mondays,
    I'll squeak and roar, and grunt without cessation,
    And utterly confound your recitation.
And, mark me! all my friends of the furry snout
        Shall join a chorus shout:

We will be heard—we'll spoil
Your wicked ruination toil.
  Insolvency must ensue
  To you, Sir, you ;
Unless you move your opposition shop,
  And let me stop.

I have no more to say :—I do not write
 In anger, but in sorrow ; I must look,
However, to my interests every night,
 And they detest your " Memorandum-book."
If we could join our forces—I should like it ;
  You do the dialogue, and I the songs.
  A voice to me belongs ;
(The Editors of the Globe and Traveller ring
With praises of it, when I hourly sing
  God save the King.)
If such a bargain could be schemed, I'd strike it!
 I think, too, I could do the Welch old man
 In the Youthful Days, if dress'd upon your plan ;
And the attorney in your Paris trip,—
  I'm large about the hip !
Now think of this !—for we cannot go on
 As next door rivals, that my mind declares :
I must be pennyless, or you be gone !
We must live separate, or else have shares.
  I am a friend or foe
  As you take this ;
 Let me your profitable hubbub miss,
Or be it " Mathews, Elephant, and Co. ! "

A NEW LIFE PRESERVER.

"Of hair-breadth 'scapes."—OTHELLO.

— ✦ —

I HAVE read somewhere of a Traveller, who carried with him a brace of pistols, a carbine, a cutlass, a dagger, and an umbrella, but was indebted for his preservation to the umbrella: it grappled with a bush, when he was rolling over a precipice. In like manner, my friend W——, though armed with a sword, rifle, and hunting-knife, owed his existence—to his wig!

He was specimen-hunting (for W—— is a first-rate naturalist), somewhere in the backwoods of America, when, happening to light upon a dense covert, there sprang out upon him,—not a panther or catamountain,—but, with terrible whoop and yell, a wild Indian,—one of a tribe then hostile to our settlers. W——'s gun was mastered in a twinkling, himself stretched on the earth, the barbarous knife, destined to make him balder than Granby's celebrated Marquis, leaped eagerly from its sheath.

Conceive the horrible weapon making its preliminary flourishes and circumgyrations; the savage features, made savager by paint and ruddle, working themselves up to a demoniacal crisis of triumphant malignity; his red right hand clutching the shearing knife; his left the frizzled top-knot; and then, the artificial scalp coming off in the Mohawk grasp!

W—— says the Indian catchpole was, for some moments, motionless, with surprise: recovering, at last, he dragged his captive along, through brake and jungle, to the encampment. A peculiar whoop soon brought the whole horde to the spot. The Indian addressed them with vehement gestures, in the course of which, W—— was again thrown down, the knife again performed its circuits, and the whole transaction was pantomimically described. All Indian sedateness and restraint were overcome. The assembly made every demonstration of wonder; and the wig was fitted on, rightly, askew, and hind part before, by a hundred pair of red hands. Captain Gulliver's glove was not a greater puzzle to the Houhyhnms. From the men, it passed to the squaws; and from them, down to the least of the urchins; W——'s head, in the meantime, frying in a midsummer sun. At length, the phenomenon returned into the hands of the chief —a venerable grey-beard : he examined it afresh, very attentively, and, after a long deliberation, maintained with true Indian silence and gravity, made a speech in his own tongue, that procured for the anxious trembling captive very unexpected honours. In fact, the whole tribe of women and warriors danced round him, with such unequivocal marks of homage, that even W—— comprehended that he was not intended for sacrifice. He was then carried in triumph to their wigwams; his body daubed with their body-colours of the most honourable patterns; and he was given to understand, that he might choose any of their mar- riageable maidens for a squaw. Availing himself of this privilege, and so becoming, by degrees, more a proficient in their language, he learned the cause of this extraordinary respect.—It was considered, that he had been a great warrior; that he had, by mis- chance of war, been overcome and tufted ; but, that, whether by valour or stratagem, each equally estimable amongst the savages, he had recovered his liberty and his scalp.

As long as W—— kept his own counsel, he was safe; but trusting his Indian Dalilah with the secret of his locks, it soon got wind amongst the squaws, and, from them, became known to the warriors and chiefs. A solemn sitting was held at midnight, by the chiefs, to consider the propriety of knocking the poor wig-owner on the head; but he had received a timely hint of their intention, and, when the tomahawks sought for him, he was far on his way, with his Life-preserver, towards a British settlement.

"A MAN'S A MAN FOR A' THAT."

A DREAM.

In the figure above,—(a medley of human faces, wherein certain features belong in common to different visages, the eyebrow of one, for instance, forming the mouth of another,)—I have tried to typify a common characteristic of dreams, namely, the entanglement of divers ideas, to the waking mind distinct or incongruous, but, by the confusion of sleep, inseparably ravelled up, and knotted into Gordian intricacies. For, as the equivocal feature, in the emblem, belongs indifferently to either countenance, but is appropriated by the head that happens to be presently the object of contemplation; so, in a dream, two separate notions

will mutually involve some convertible incident, that
becomes, by turns, a symptom of both in general, or
of either in particular. Thus are begotten the most
extravagant associations of thoughts and images,—unnatural connexions, like those marriages of forbidden
relationships, where mothers become cousins to their
own sons or daughters, and quite as bewildering as
such genealogical embarrassments.

I had a dismal dream once, of this nature, that will
serve well for an illustration, and which originated in
the failure of my first, and last, attempt as a dramatic
writer. Many of my readers, if I were to name the
piece in question, would remember its signal con-
demnation. As soon as the Tragedy of my Tragedy
was completed, I got into a coach, and rode home.
My nerves were quivering with shame and mortifica-
tion. I tried to compose myself over "Paradise Lost,"
but it failed to soothe me. I flung myself into bed,
and at length slept; but the disaster of the night still
haunted my dreams: I was again in the accursed
theatre, but with a difference. It was a compound of
the Drury-Lane Building, and Pandemonium. There
were the old shining green pillars, on either side of
the stage, but, above, a sublimer dome than ever
overhung mortal playhouse. The wonted familiars
were in keeping of the fore-spoken seats, but the first
companies they admitted were new and strange to the
place. The first and second tiers,

"With dreadful faces thronged, and fiery arms,"

showed like those purgatorial circles sung of by the
ancient Florentine. Satan was in the stage-box. The
pit, dismally associated with its bottomless name-sake,
was peopled with fiends. Mehu scowled from the

I 2

critic's seat.   Belial, flushed with wine, led on with
shout and catcall the uproar of the one-shilling infer-
nals.   My hair stood upright with dread and horror;
I had an appalling sense, that more than my dramatic
welfare was at stake:—that it was to be not a purely
literary ordeal.   An alarming figure, sometimes a newspaper reporter, sometimes a devil, so prevaricating are
the communications of sleep, was sitting, with his
note-book, at my side.   My play began.   As it proceeded, sounds indescribable arose from the infernal
auditory, increasing till the end of the first act.   The
familiar cry of " Chuse any oranges," was then inter-
mingled with the murmurings of demons.   The tumult grew with the progress of the play.   The last
act passed in dumb show, the horned monsters bellow-
ing, throughout, like the wild bulls of Bashan.   Prongs
and flesh-hooks showered upon the stage.   Mrs. Sid-
dons—the human nature thus jumbling with the
diabolical—was struck by a brimstone ball.   Her lofty
brother, robed in imperial purple, came forward towards the orchestra, to remonstrate, and was received
like the Arch-devil in the Poem:

> " he hears
> On all sides, from innumerable tongues,
> A dismal universal hiss, the sound
> Of public scorn."

He bowed to the sense of the house, and withdrew.
My doom was sealed; the recording devil noted down
my sentence.   A suffocating vapour, now smelling of
sulphur, and now of gas, issued from the unquenchable
stage lamps.   The flames of the Catalonian Castle.
burning in the back scene, in compliance with the
catastrophe of the piece, blazed up with horrible im-

port. My flesh crept all over me. I thought of the everlasting torments, and, at the next moment, of the morrow's paragraphs. I shrank from the comments of the Morning Post, and, the hot marl of Malebolge The sins of authorship had confounded themselves, inextricably, with the mortal sins of the law. I could not disentangle my own from my play's perdition. I was damned: but whether spiritually or dramatically, the twilight intelligence of a dream was not clear enough to determine.

Another sample, wherein the preliminaries of the dream involved one portion, and implicitly forbade the other half of the conclusion, was more whimsical. It occurred when I was on the eve of marriage, a season, when, if lovers sleep sparingly, they dream profusely. A very brief slumber sufficed to carry me in the night-coach to Bognor. It had been concerted, between Honoria and myself, that we should pass the honeymoon at some such place upon the coast. The purpose of my solitary journey was to procure an appropriate dwelling, and which, we had agreed, should be a little pleasant house, with an indispensable look-out upon the sea. I chose one, accordingly; a pretty villa, with bow-windows, and a prospect delightfully marine. The ocean-murmur sounded incessantly from the beach. A decent elderly body, in decayed sables, undertook, on her part, to promote the comforts of the occupants by every suitable attention, and, as she assured me, at a very reasonable rate. So far, the nocturnal faculty had served me truly. A day-dream could not have proceeded more orderly; but, alas! just here, when the dwelling was selected, the sea-view secured, the rent agreed upon, when every thing was plausible, consistent, and rational, the incoherent

fancy crept in and confounded all,—by marrying me
to the old woman of the house!

A large proportion of my dreams have, like the
preceding, an origin, more or less remote, in some
actual occurrence. But, from all my observation and
experience, the popular notion is a mistaken one, that
our dreams take their subject and colour from the
business or meditations of the day. It is true, that
sleep frequently gives back real images and actions,
like a mirror; but the reflection returns at a longer
interval. It extracts from pages of some standing,
like the " Retrospective Review." The mind, released
from its connexion with external associations, flies off,
gladly, to novel speculations. The soul does not
carry its tasks out of school. The novel, read upon
the pillow, is of no more influence than the bride-
cake laid beneath it. The charms of Di Vernon have
faded with me, into a vision of Dr. Faustus; the
bridal dance and festivities, into a chase by a mad
bullock.

The sleeper, like the felon, at the putting on of the
night-cap, is about to be turned off from the affairs of
this world. The material scaffold sinks under him;
he drops—as it is expressively called—asleep; and
the spirit is transported, we know not whither!

I should like to know, that, by any earnest application of thought, we could impress its subject upon
the midnight blank. It would be worth a day's devo-
tion to Milton,—"from morn till noon, from noon till
dewy eve,"—to obtain but one glorious vision from
the " Paradise Lost;" to Spenser, to purchase but one
magical reflection—a Fata Morgana, of the " Faery
Queen ! " I have heard it affirmed, indeed, by a
gentleman, an especial advocate of Early Rising, that

he could procure whatever dream he wished; but I
disbelieve it, or he would pass far more hours than he
does in bed. If it were possible, by any process, to
bespeak the night's entertainment, the theatres, for
me, might close their uninviting doors. Who would
care to sit at the miserable stage-parodies of " Lear,"
" Hamlet," and " Othello ;" to say nothing of the
" Tempest," or the " Midsummer Night's Phantasy,"
—that could command the representation of either of
those noble Dramas, with all the sublime personations,
the magnificent scenery, and awful reality, of a dream ?

For horrible fancies, merely, nightmares and incubi,
there is a recipe extant, that is currently attributed
to the late Mr. Fuseli. I mean, a supper of raw
pork ; but, as I never slept after it, I cannot speak as
to the effect.

Opium, I have never tried, and, therefore, have
never experienced such magnificent visions as are
described by its eloquent historian. I have never
been buried for ages under pyramids; and yet, methinks,
have suffered agonies as intense as *his* could be, from
the common-place inflictions. For example, a night
spent in the counting of interminable numbers,—an
Inquisitorial penance, — everlasting tedium, — the
Mind's tread-mill !

Another writer, in recording his horrible dreams,
describes himself to have been sometimes an animal
pursued by hounds; sometimes a bird, torn in pieces
by eagles. They are flat contradictions of my Theory
of Dreams. Such Ovidian Metamorphoses never yet
entered into my experience. I never translate myself.
I must know the taste of rape and hempseed, and
have cleansed my gizzard with small gravel, before
even Fancy can turn me into a bird. I must have

another noul upon my shoulders, ere I can feel a
longing for "a bottle of chopt hay, or your good dried
oats." My own habits and prejudices, all the
symptoms of my identity, cling to me in my dreams.
It never happened to me to fancy myself a child or a
woman, dwarf or giant, stone-blind, or deprived of any
sense.

And here, the latter part of the sentence reminds
me of an interesting question, on this subject, that has
greatly puzzled me; and of which I should be glad to
obtain a satisfactory solution, viz.—How does a blind
man dream? I mean a person with the opaque
chrystal from his birth. He is defective in that very
faculty, which, of all others, is most active in those
night-passages, thence emphatically called Visions.
He has had no acquaintance with external images, and
has, therefore, none of those transparent pictures,
that, like the slides of a magic-lantern, pass before the
mind's eye, and are projected by the inward spiritual
light upon the utter blank. His imagination must be
like an imperfect kaleidoscope, totally unfurnished
with those parti-coloured fragments, whereof the
complete instrument makes such interminable combinations. It is difficult to conceive such a man's
dream.

Is it, a still benighted wandering,—a pitch-dark
night progress, made known to him by the consciousness of the remaining senses? Is he still pulled
through the universal blank, by an invisible power, as
it were, at the nether end of the string?—regaled,
sometimes, with celestial voluntaries and unknown
mysterious fragrances, answering to our more romantic
flights; at other times, with homely voices and more
familiar odours; here, of rank-smelling cheeses; there,

of pungent pickles or aromatic drugs, hinting his
progress through a metropolitan street? Does he over
again enjoy the grateful roundness of those substantial droppings from the invisible passenger,—palpable
deposits of an abstract benevolence,—or, in his nightmares, suffer anew those painful concussions and
corporeal buffetings, from that (to him) obscure evil
principle, the Parish Beadle?

This question I am happily enabled to resolve,
through the information of the oldest of those blind
Tobits that stand in fresco against Bunhill Wall; the
same who made that notable comparison, of scarlet, to
the sound of a trumpet. As I understood him,
harmony, with the gravel-blind, is prismatic as well
as chromatic. To use his own illustration, a wall-
eyed man has a *palette* in his ear, as well as in his
mouth. Some stone-blinds, indeed, dull dogs, without
any *ear* for colour, profess to distinguish the different
hues and shades, by the touch, but *that*, he said, was
a slovenly uncertain method, and in the chief article
of Paintings not allowed to be exercised.

On my expressing some natural surprise at the apti-
tude of his celebrated comparison,—a miraculous close
likening, to my mind, of the known to the unknown,
—he told me, the instance was nothing, for the least
discriminative among them could distinguish the
scarlet colour of the mail-guards' liveries, by the
sound of their horns; but there were others, so acute
their faculty! that they could tell the very features
and complexion of their relatives and familiars, by the
mere tone of their voices. I was much gratified with
this explanation; for I confess, hitherto, I was always
extremely puzzled by that narrative in the "Tatler,"
of a young gentleman's behaviour after the operation

of couching, and especially at the wonderful prompt-
ness with which he distinguished his father from his
mother,—his mistress from her maid.   But it appears
that the blind are not so blind as they have been
esteemed in the vulgar notion.   What they cannot
get in one way they obtain in another: they, in fact,
realise what the author of Hudibras has ridiculed as a
fiction, for they set up

> " communities of senses,
> To chop and change intelligences,
> As Rosicrucian Virtuosis
> Can *see with ears*—and hear with noses."

SPRING AND FALL.

THE IRISH SCHOOLMASTER.

— ✦ —

I.

Alack ! 'tis melancholy theme to think
How Learning doth in rugged states abide,
And, like her bashful owl, obscurely blink,
In pensive glooms and corners, scarcely spied;
Not, as in Founders'Halls and domes of pride,
Served with grave homage, like a tragic queen,
But with one lonely priest compell'd to hide,
In midst of foggy moors and mosses green,
In that clay cabin hight the College of Kilreen !

II.

This College looketh South and West alsoe,
Because it hath a cast in windows twain ;
Crazy and crack'd they be, and wind doth blow
Thorough transparent holes in every pane,
Which Dan, with many paines, makes whole again
With nether garments, which his thrift doth teach,
To stand for glass, like pronouns, and when rain
Stormeth, he puts, "once more unto the breach,"
Outside and in, tho' broke, yet so he mendeth each.

III.

And in the midst a little door there is,
Whereon a board that doth congratulate
With painted letters, red as blood I wis,
Thus written,
        "CHILDREN TAKEN IN TO BATE,"
And oft, indeed, the inward of that gate,
Most ventriloque, doth utter tender squeak,
And moans of infants that bemoan their fate,
In midst of sounds of Latin, French, and Greek,
Which, all i' the Irish tongue, he teacheth them to speak.

IV.

For some are meant to right illegal wrongs,
And some for Doctors of Divinitie,
Whom he doth teach to murder the dead tongues,
And soe win academical degree;
But some are bred for service of the sea,
Howbeit, their store of learning is but small,
For mickle waste he counteth it would be
To stock a head with bookish wares at all,
Only to be knocked off by ruthless cannon ball.

V.

Six babes he sways,—some little and some big,
Divided into classes six;—alsoe,
He keeps a parlour boarder of a pig,
That in the College fareth to and fro,
And picketh up the urchins' crumbs below,—
And eke the learned rudiments they scan,
And thus his A, B, C, doth wisely know,—
Hereafter to be shown in caravan,
And raise the wonderment of many a learned man.

VI.

Alsoe, he schools some tame familiar fowls,
Whereof, above his head, some two or three
Sit darkly squatting, like Minerva's owls,
But on the branches of no living tree,
And overlook the learned family;
While, sometimes, Partlet, from her gloomy perch,
Drops feather on the nose of Dominie,
Meanwhile, with serious eye, he makes research
In leaves of that sour tree of knowledge—now a birch.

VII.

No chair he hath, the awful Pedagogue,
Such as would magisterial hams imbed,
But sitteth lowly on a beechen log,
Secure in high authority and dread:
Large, as a dome for learning, seems his head,
And like Apollo's, all beset with rays,
Because his locks are so unkempt and red,
And stand abroad in many several ways:—
No laurel crown he wears, howbeit his cap is baize,

VIII.

And, underneath, a pair of shaggy brows
O'erhang as many eyes of gizzard hue,
That inward giblet of a fowl, which shows
A mongrel tint, that is ne brown ne blue;
His nose,—it is a coral to the view;
Well nourish'd with Pierian Potheen,—
For much he loves his native mountain dew;—
But to depict the dye would lack, I ween,
A bottle-red, in terms, as well as bottle-green.

IX.

As for his coat, 'tis such a jerkin short
As Spencer had, ere he composed his Tales;
But underneath he hath no vest, nor aught,
So that the wind his airy breast assails;
Below, he wears the nether garb of males,
Of crimson plush, but non-plushed at the knee; —
Thence further down the native red prevails,
Of his own naked fleecy hosierie :—
Two sandals, without soles, complete his cap-a-pee.

X.

Nathless, for dignity, he now doth lap
His function in a magisterial gown,
That shows more countries in it than a map,—
Blue tinct, and red, and green, and russet brown,
Besides some blots, standing for country-town;
And eke some rents, for streams and rivers wide;
But, sometimes, bashful when he looks adown,
He turns the garment of the other side,
Hopeful that so the holes may never be espied!

XI.

And soe he sits, amidst the little pack,
That look for shady or for sunny noon,
Within his visage, like an almanack,—
His quiet smile foretelling gracious boon :
But when his mouth droops down, like rainy moon,
With horrid chill each little heart unwarms,
Knowing, that infant show'rs will follow soon,
And with forebodings of near wrath and storms
They sit, like timid hares, all trembling on their forms.

XII.

Ah! luckless wight, who cannot then repeat
" Corduroy Colloquy,"—or " Ki, Kæ, Kod,"—
Full soon his tears shall make his turfy seat
More sodden, tho' already made of sod,
For Dan shall whip him with the word of God,—
Severe by rule, and not by nature mild,
He never spoils the child and spares the rod,
But spoils the rod and never spares the child,
And soe with holy rule deems he is reconcil'd.

XIII.

But, surely, the just sky will never wink
At men who take delight in childish throe,
And stripe the nether-urchin like a pink
Or tender hyacinth, inscribed with woe;
Such bloody Pedagogues, when they shall know,
By useless birches, that forlorn recess,
Which is no holiday, in Pit below,
Will hell not seem designed for their distress,—
A melancholy place, that is all bottomlesse?

XIV.

Yet would the Muse not chide the wholesome use
Of needful discipline, in due degree.
Devoid of sway, what wrongs will time produce,
Whene'er the twig untrain'd grows up a tree,
This shall a Carder, that a Whiteboy be,
Ferocious leaders of atrocious bands,
And Learning's help be used for infamie,
By lawless clerks, that, with their bloody hands,
In murder'd English write Rock's murderous com-
mands.

XV.

But ah! what shrilly cry doth now alarm
The sooty fowls that doz'd upon the beam,
All sudden fluttering from the brandish'd arm,
And cackling chorus with the human scream;
Meanwhile, the scourge plies that unkindly scam
In Phelim's brogues, which bares his naked skin,
Like traitor gap in warlike fort, I deem,
That falsely lets the fierce besieger in,
Nor seeks the Pedagogue by other course to win.

XVI.

No parent dear he hath to heed his cries;—
Alas! his parent dear is far aloof,
And deep his Seven-Dial cellar lies,
Killed by kind cudgel-play, or gin of proof,
Or climbeth, catwise, on some London roof,
Singing, perchance, a lay of Erin's Isle,
Or, whilst he labours, weaves a fancy-woof,
Dreaming he sees his home,—his Phelim smile;
Ah me! that luckless imp, who weepeth all the while!

XVII.

Ah! who can paint that hard and heavy time,
When first the scholar lists in learning's train,
And mounts her rugged steep, enforc'd to climb,
Like sooty imp, by sharp posterior pain,
From bloody twig, and eke that Indian cane,
Wherein, alas! no sugar'd juices dwell?
For this, the while one stripling's sluices drain,
Another weepeth over chilblains fell,
Always upon the heel, yet never to be well!

XVIII.

Anon a third, for his delicious root,
Late ravish'd from his tooth by elder chit,
So soon is human violence afoot,
So hardly is the harmless biter bit!
Meanwhile, the tyrant, with untimely wit
And mouthing face, derides the small one's moan,
Who, all lamenting for his loss, doth sit,
Alack,—mischance comes seldomtimes alone,
But aye the worried dog must rue more curs than one.

XIX.

For lo! the Pedagogue, with sudden drub,
Smites his scald head, that is already sore,—
Superfluous wound,—such is Misfortune's rub!
Who straight makes answer with redoubled roar,
And sheds salt tears twice faster than before,
That still, with backward fist, he strives to dry;
Washing, with brackish moisture, o'er and o'er,
His muddy cheek, that grows more foul thereby,
Till all his rainy face looks grim as rainy sky.

XX.

So Dan, by dint of noise, obtains a peace,
And with his natural untender knack,
By new distress, bids former grievance cease,
Like tears dried up with rugged huckaback,
That sets the mournful visage all awrack;
Yet soon the childish countenance will shine
Even as thorough storms the soonest slack,
For grief and beef in adverse ways incline,
This keeps, and that decays, when duly soak'd in brine.

K

XXI.

Now all is hushed, and, with a look profound,
The Dominie lays ope the learned page ;
(So be it called) although he doth expound
Without a book, both Greek and Latin sage ;
Now telleth he of Rome's rude infant age,
How Romulus was bred in savage wood,
By wet-nurse wolf, devoid of wolfish rage ;
And laid foundation-stone of walls of mud,
But watered it, alas! with warm fraternal blood.

XXII.

Anon, he turns to that Homeric war,
How Troy was sieged like Londonderry town ;
And stout Achilles, at his jaunting-car,
Dragged mighty Hector with a bloody crown :
And eke the bard, that sung of their renown,
In garb of Greece most beggar-like and torn,
He paints, with colly, wand'ring up and down :
Because, at once, in seven cities born ;
And so, of parish rights, was, all his days, forlorn.

XXIII.

Anon, through old Mythology he goes,
Of gods defunct, and all their pedigrees,
But shuns their scandalous amours, and shows
How Plato wise, and clear-ey'd Socrates,
Confess'd not to those heathen hes and shes ;
But thro' the clouds of the Olympic cope
Beheld St. Peter, with his holy keys,
And own'd their love was naught, and bow'd to Pope,
Whilst all their purblind race in Pagan mist did grope.

XXIV.

From such quaint themes he turns, at last, aside,
To new philosophies, that still are green,
And shows what rail-roads have been track'd to guide
The wheels of great political machine;
If English corn should grow abroad, I ween,
And gold be made of gold, or paper sheet;
How many pigs be born to each spalpeen;
And ah! how man shall thrive beyond his meat,—
With twenty souls alive, to one square rod of peat!

XXV.

Here, he makes end; and all the fry of youth,
That stood around with serious look intense,
Close up again their gaping eyes and mouth,
Which they had opened to his eloquence,
As if their hearing were a threefold sense;
But now the current of his words is done,
And whether any fruits shall spring from thence,
In future time, with any mother's son!
It is a thing, God wot! that can be told by none.

XXVI.

Now by the creeping shadows of the noon,
The hour is come to lay aside their lore;
The cheerful Pedagogue perceives it soon,
And cries, " Begone!" unto the imps,—and four
Snatch their two hats, and struggle for the door,
Like ardent spirits vented from a cask,
All blythe and boisterous,—but leave two more,
With Reading made Uneasy for a task,
To weep, whilst all their mates in merry sunshine bask.

K 2

XXVII.

Like sportive Elfins, on the verdant sod,
With tender moss so sleekly overgrown,
That doth not hurt, but kiss, the sole unshod,
So soothly kind is Erin to her own!
And one, at Hare and Hound, plays all alone,—
For Phelim's gone to tend his step-dame's cow;
Ah! Phelim's step-dame is a canker'd crone!
Whilst other twain play at an Irish row,
And, with shillelah small, break one another's brow!

XXVIII.

But careful Dominie, with ceaseless thrift,
Now changeth ferula for rural hoe;
But, first of all, with tender hand doth shift
His college gown, because of solar glow,
And hangs it on a bush, to scare the crow:
Meanwhile, he plants in earth the dappled bean,
Or trains the young potatoes all a-row,
Or plucks the fragrant leek for pottage green,
With that crisp curly herb, call'd Kale in Aberdeen.

XXIX.

And so he wisely spends the fruitful hours,
Link'd each to each by labour, like a bee;
Or rules in Learning's hall, or trims her bow'rs;—
Would there were many more such wights as he,
To sway each capital academie
Of Cam and Isis; for, alack! at each
There dwells, I wot, some dronish Dominie,
That does no garden work, nor yet doth teach,
But wears a floury head, and talks in flow'ry speech!

FAITHLESS NELLY GRAY.

A PATHETIC BALLAD.

I.

BEN Battle was a soldier bold,
　And used to war's alarms:
But a cannon-ball took off his legs,
　So he laid down his arms!

II.

Now as they bore him off the field,
　Said he, " Let others shoot,
For here I leave my second leg,
　And the Forty-second Foot!"

III.

The army-surgeons made him limbs:
　Said he,—" They're only pegs:
But there's as wooden members quite,
　As represent my legs!"

IV.

Now Ben he loved a pretty maid,
　Her name was Nelly Gray;
So he went to pay her his devours,
　When he'd devoured his pay!

V.

But when he called on Nelly Gray,
   She made him quite a scoff;
And when she saw his wooden legs,
   Began to take them off!

VI.

"O Nelly Gray! O, Nelly Gray!
   Is this your love so warm?
The love that loves a scarlet coat,
   Should be more uniform!"

VII.

Said she, "I loved a soldier once,
   For he was blythe and brave;
But I will never have a man
   With both legs in the grave!

VIII.

"Before you had those timber toes,
   Your love I did allow,
But then, you know, you stand upon
   Another footing now!"

IX.

"O, Nelly Gray! O, Nelly Gray!
   For all your jeering speeches,
At duty's call, I left my legs
   In Badajos's *breaches!*"

X.

"Why, then," said she, "you've lost the feet
   Of legs in war's alarms,
And now you cannot wear your shoes
   Upon your feats of arms!"

XI.

" O, false and fickle Nelly Gray !
    I know why you refuse :—
Though I've no feet—some other man
    Is standing in my shoes !

XII.

I wish I ne'er had seen your face ;
    But, now, a long farewell !
For you will be my death ;—alas !
    You will not be my *Nell !*"

XIII.

Now when he went from Nelly Gray,
    His heart so heavy got—
And life was such a burthen grown,
    It made him take a knot !

XIV.

So round his melancholy neck,
    A rope he did entwine,
And, for his second time in life,
    Enlisted in the Line !

XV.

One end he tied around a beam,
    And then removed his pegs,
And, as his legs were off,—of course,
    He soon was off his legs !

XVI.

And there he hung, till he was dead
    As any nail in town,—
For though distress had cut him up,
    It could not cut him down !

XVII.

A dozen men sat on his corpse,
　To find out why he died—
And they buried Ben in four cross-roads,
　With a *stake* in his inside!

"DE GUSTIBUS NON EST DISPUTANDUM."

THE SEA-SPELL.

" *Cauld, cauld,* he lies beneath the deep."

Old Scotch Ballad

—◆—

I.

It was a jolly mariner!
The tallest man of three,—
He loosed his sail against the wind,
And turned his boat to sea:
The ink-black sky told every eye,
A storm was soon to be!

II.

But still that jolly mariner
Took in no reef at all,
For, in his pouch, confidingly,
He wore a baby's caul;
A thing, as gossip-nurses know,
That always brings a squall!

III.

His hat was new, or, newly glaz'd,
Shone **brightly** in the sun;
His jacket, like a mariner's,
True blue as e'er was spun;
His ample trowsers, like Saint Paul,
Bore forty stripes save one.

IV.

And now the fretting foaming tide
He steer'd away to cross;
The bounding pinnace play'd a game
Of dreary pitch and toss;
A game that, on the good dry land,
Is apt to bring a loss!

V.

Good Heaven befriend that little boat,
And guide her on her way!
A boat, they say, has canvass wings,
But cannot fly away!
Though, like a merry singing-bird,
She sits upon the spray!

VI.

Still east by south the little boat,
With tawny sail, kept beating:
Now out of sight, between two waves,
Now o'er th' horizon fleeting:
Like greedy swine that feed on mast,—
The waves her mast seem'd eating!

VII.

The sullen sky grew black above,
The wave as black beneath;
Each roaring billow show'd full soon
A white and foamy wreath;
Like angry dogs that snarl at first,
And then display their teeth.

VIII.

The boatman looked against the wind,
The mast began to creak,
The wave, per saltum, came and dried,
In salt, upon his cheek!
The pointed wave against him rear'd,
As if it own'd a pique!

IX.

Nor rushing wind, nor gushing wave,
That boatman could alarm,
But still he stood away to sea,
And trusted in his charm;
He thought by purchase he was safe,
And arm'd against all harm!

X.

Now thick and fast and far aslant,
The stormy rain came pouring,
He heard, upon the sandy bank,
The distant breakers roaring,—
A groaning intermitting sound,
Like Gog and Magog snoring!

XI.

The sea-fowl shriek'd around the mast,
Ahead the grampus tumbled,
And far off, from a copper cloud,
The hollow thunder rumbled;
It would have quail'd another heart,
But his was never humbled.

XII.

For why ? he had that infant's caul ;
And wherefore should he dread ?
Alas! alas! he little thought,
Before the ebb-tide sped,—
That like that infant, he should die,
And with a watery head !

XIII.

The rushing brine flowed in apace ;
His boat had ne'er a deck ;
Fate seem'd to call him on, and he
Attended to her beck ;
And so he went, still trusting on,
Though reckless—to his wreck !

XIV.

For as he left his helm, to heave
The ballast-bags a-weather,
Three monstrous seas came roaring on,
Like lions leagued together.
The two first waves the little boat
Swam over like a feather.—

XV.

The two first waves were past and gone,
And sinking in her wake ;
The hugest still came leaping on,
And hissing like a snake ;
Now helm a-lee ! for through the midst,
The monster he must take !

XVI.

Ah, me! it was a dreary mount!
Its base as black as night,
Its top of pale and livid green,
Its crest of awful white,
Like Neptune with a leprosy,—
And so it rear'd upright!

XVII.

With quaking sails, the little boat
Climb'd up the foaming heap;
With quaking sails it paused awhile,
At balance on the steep;
Then rushing down the nether slope,
Plunged with a dizzy sweep!

XVIII.

Look, how a horse, made mad with fear,
Disdains his careful guide;
So now the headlong headstrong boat,
Unmanaged, turns aside,
And straight presents her reeling flank
Against the swelling tide!

XIX.

The gusty wind assaults the sail;
Her ballast lies a-lee!
The sheet's to windward taught and stiff!
Oh! the Lively—where is she?
Her capsiz'd keel is in the foam,
Her pennon's in the sea!

XX.

The wild gull, sailing overhead,
Three times beheld emerge
The head of that bold mariner,
And then she screamed his dirge!
For he had sunk within his grave,
Lapp'd in a shroud of surge!

XXI.

The ensuing wave, with horrid foam,
Rush'd o'er and covered all,—
The jolly boatman's drowning scream
Was smother'd by the squall,—
Heaven never heard his cry, nor did
The ocean heed his *caul*.

FANCY PORTRAIT:—CAPTAIN HEAD.

FANCY PORTRAITS.

THE BARD OF HOPE.

—◆—

MANY authors preface their works with a portrait, and it saves the reader a deal of speculation. The world loves to know something of the features of its favourites;—it likes the Geniuses to appear bodily, as well as the Genii. We may estimate the liveliness of this curiosity, by the abundance of portraits, masks, busts, china and plaster casts, that are extant, of great

or would-be great people. As soon as a gentleman
has proved, in print, that he really has a head,
—a score of artists begin to brush at it.   The
literary lions have no peace to their manes.   Sir
Walter is eternally sitting like Theseus to some
painter or other;—and the late Lord Byron threw
out more heads before he died than Hydra.   The first
novel of Mr. Galt had barely been announced in the
second edition, when he was requested to allow himself to be taken "in one minute;"—Mr. Geoffrey
Crayon was no sooner known to be Mr. Washington
Irving, than he was waited upon with a sheet of paper
and a pair of scissors.

The whole world, in fact, is one Lavater :—it likes
to find its prejudices confirmed by the Hook nose of
the Author of Sayings and Doings—or the lines and
angles in the honest face of Izaak Walton.   It is
gratified in dwelling on the repulsive features of a
Newgate ordinary; and would be disappointed to
miss the seraphic expression on the Author of the
Angel of the World.   The Old Bailey jurymen are
physiognomists to a fault; and if a rope can transform
a malefactor into an Adonis, a hard gallows face as
often brings the malefactor to the rope.   A low forehead is enough to bring down its head to the dust.
A well-favoured man meets with good countenance;
but when people are plain and hard-featured (like the
poor, for instance,) we grind their faces; an expression, I am convinced, that refers to physiognomical
theory.

For my part, I confess a sympathy with the common
failing.   I take likings and dislikings, as some play
music,—at sight.   The polar attractions and repul-
sions insisted on by the phrenologist, affect me not;

but I am not proof against a pleasant or villainous set of features. Sometimes, I own, I am led by the nose, (not my own, but that of the other party)—in my prepossessions.

ANACREON JUNIOR.

My curiosity does not object to the disproportionate number of portraits in the annual exhibition,—nor grudge the expense of engraving a gentleman's head and shoulders. Like Judith, and the daughter of Herodias, I have a taste for a head in a plate, and accede cheerfully to the charge of the charger. A book without a portrait of the author, is worse than anonymous. As in a church-yard, you may look on any number of ribs and shin-bones, as so many sticks merely, without interest; but if there should chance to be a skull near hand, it claims the relics at once,—so it is with the author's head-piece in front of his pages. The portrait claims the work. The Arcadia, for instance, I know is none of mine—it

L

belongs to that young fair gentleman, in armour, with a ruff.

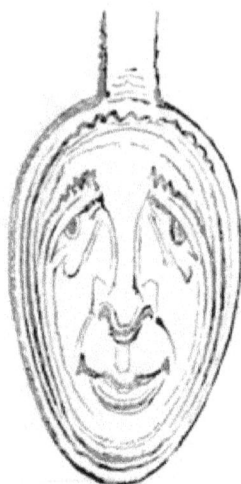

MR. BOWLES.

So necessary it is for me to have an outward visible sign of the inward spiritual poet or philosopher, that in default of an authentic resemblance, I cannot help forging for him an effigy in my mind's eye,—a Fancy portrait. A few examples of contemporaries I have sketched down, but my collection is far from complete.

THE AUTHOR OF BROAD GRINS.

How have I longed to glimpse, in fancy, the Great
Unknown!—the Roe of Literature!—but he keeps
his head, like Ben Lomond, enveloped in a cloud.
How have I sighed for a beau ideal of the author of
Christabel, and the Ancient Marinere!—but I have
been mocked with a dozen images, confusing each
other, and indistinct as water is in water. My only
clear revelation was a pair of Hessian boots, highly
polished, or what the ingenious Mr. Warren would
denominate his "Aids to Reflection!"

MR. CRABBE.

I was more certain of the figure at least of Dr.
Kitchener, (p. 26) though I had a misgiving about his
features, which made me have recourse to a substitute
for his head. Moore's profile struck me over a bottle
after dinner, and the countenance of Mr. Bowles
occurred to me as in a mirror,—by a tea-table suggestion; Colman's at the same service;—and Mr.

Crabbe entered my mind's eye with the supper. But the Bard of Hope—the Laureate of promise and expectation,—occurred to me at no meal-time. We all know how Hope feeds her own.

I had a lively image of the celebrated Denon, in a Midnight dream (p. 78) and made out the full length of the juvenile Graham, from a hint of Mr. Hilton's.

At a future season, I hope to complete my gallery of Fancy-Portraits.

END OF THE FIRST SERIES.

WHIMS AND ODDITIES.

SECOND SERIES.

" What Demon hath possessed thee, that thou wilt never forsake that
impertinent custom of punning?"

SCRIBLERUS.

IN the absence of better fiddles, I have ventured to come forward again with my little kit of fancies. I trust it will not be found an unworthy sequel to my first performance; indeed, I have done my best, in the New Series, innocently to imitate a practice that prevails abroad in duelling—I mean, that of the Seconds giving Satisfaction.

The kind indulgence that welcomed my Volume heretofore, prevents me from reiterating the same apologies. The Public have learned, by this time, from my rude designs, that I am no great artist, and from my text, that I am no great author, but humbly equivocating, bat-like, between the two kinds;—though

proud to partake in any characteristic of either. As
for the first particular, my hope persuades me that
my illustrations cannot have degenerated, so ably as I
have been seconded by Mr. Edward Willis, who, like
the humane Walter, has befriended my offspring in
the Wood.

In the literary part I have to plead guilty, as usual,
to some verbal misdemeanors ; for which, I must
leave my defence to Dean Swift, and the other great
European and Oriental Pundits. Let me suggest,
however, that a pun is somewhat like a cherry : though
there may be a slight outward indication of partition
—of duplicity of meaning—yet no gentleman need
make two bites at it against his own pleasure. To
accommodate certain readers, notwithstanding, I have
refrained from putting the majority in italics. It is
not every one, I am aware, that can Toler-ate a pun
like my Lord Norbury.

WHIMS AND ODDITIES.

SECOND SERIES.

BIANCA'S DREAM.

A VENETIAN STORY.

I.

Bianca!—fair Bianca!—who could dwell
  With safety on her dark and hazel gaze,
Nor find there lurk'd in it a witching spell,
  Fatal to balmy nights and blessed days?
The peaceful breath that made the bosom swell,
  She turn'd to gas, and set it in a blaze;
Each eye of hers had Love's Eupyrion in it,
That he could light his link at in a minute.

II.

So that, wherever in her charms she shone,
  A thousand breasts were kindled into flame;
Maidens who cursed her looks forgot their own,
  And beaux were turn'd to flambeaux where she came;
All hearts indeed were conquer'd but her own,
  Which none could ever temper down or tame:
In short, to take our haberdasher's hints,
She might have written over it,—"from Flints."

III.

She was, in truth, the wonder of her sex,
    At least in Venice—where with eyes of brown
Tenderly languid, ladies seldom vex
    An amorous gentle with a needless frown ;
Where gondolas convey guitars by pecks,
    And love at casements climbeth up and down,
Whom for his tricks and custom in that kind,
Some have consider'd a Venetian blind.

IV.

Howbeit, this difference was quickly taught,
    Amongst more youths who had this cruel jailor,
To hapless Julio—all in vain he sought
    With each new moon his hatter and his tailor ;
In vain the richest padusoy he bought,
    And went in bran new beaver to assail her—
As if to show that Love had made him *smart*
All over—and not merely round his heart.

V.

In vain he labour'd thro' the sylvan park
    Bianca haunted in—that where she came,
Her learned eyes in wandering might mark
    The twisted cipher of her maiden name,
Wholesomely going thro' a course of bark :
    No one was touch'd or troubled by his flame,
Except the Dryads, those old maids that grow
In trees,—like wooden dolls in embryo.

VI.

In vain complaining elegies he writ,
    And taught his tuneful instrument to grieve,
And sang in quavers how his heart was split,
    Constant beneath her lattice with each eve ;

She mock'd his wooing with her wicked wit,
   And slash'd his suit so that it match'd his sleeve,
Till he grew silent at the vesper star,
And quite despairing, hamstring'd his guitar.

VII.

Bianca's heart was coldly frosted o'er
   With snows unmelting—an eternal sheet,
But his was red within him, like the core
   Of old Vesuvius, with perpetual heat ;
And oft he long'd internally to pour
   His flames and glowing lava at her feet,
But when his burnings he began to spout,
She stopp'd his mouth, and put the *crater* out.

VIII.

Meanwhile he wasted in the eyes of men,
   So thin, he seem'd a sort of skeleton-key
Suspended at death's door—so pale—and then
   He turn'd as nervous as an aspen tree ;
The life of man is three-score years and ten,
   But he was perishing at twenty-three,
For people truly said, as grief grew stronger,
" It could not shorten his poor life—much longer."

IX.

For why, he neither slept, nor drank, nor fed,
   Nor relish'd any kind of mirth below ;
Fire in his heart, and frenzy in his head,
   Love had become his universal foe,
Salt in his sugar—nightmare in his bed.
   At last, no wonder wretched Julio,
A sorrow-ridden thing, in utter dearth
Of hope—made up his mind to cut her girth !

X.

For hapless lovers always died of old,
    Sooner than chew reflection's bitter cud;
So Thisbe stuck herself, what time 'tis told,
    The tender-hearted mulberries wept blood;
And so poor Sappho, when her boy was cold,
    Drown'd her salt tear-drops in a salter flood,
Their fame still breathing, tho' their breath be past,
For those old *suitors* lived beyond their last.

XI.

So Julio went to drown,—when life was dull,
    But took his corks, and merely had a bath;
And once, he pull'd a trigger at his skull,
    But merely broke a window in his wrath;
And once, his hopeless being to annul,
    He tied a pack-thread to a beam of lath,
A line so ample, 'twas a query whether
'Twas meant to be a halter or a tether.

XII.

Smile not in scorn, that Julio did not thrust
    His sorrows thro'—'tis horrible to die!
And come down with our little all of dust,
    That dun of all the duns to satisfy:
To leave life's pleasant city as we must,
    In Death's most dreary spunging-house to lie,
Where even all our personals must go
To pay the debt of Nature that we owe!

XIII.

So Julio lived:—'twas nothing but a pet
    He took at life—a momentary spite;
Besides, he hoped that time would some day get
    The better of love's flame, however bright;

A thing that time has never compass'd yet,
  For love, we know, is an immortal light;
Like that old fire, that, quite beyond a doubt,
Was always in,—for none have found it out.

XIV.

Meanwhile, Bianca dream'd—'twas once when Night
  Along the darken'd plain began to creep,
Like a young Hottentot, whose eyes are bright,
  Altho' in skin as sooty as a sweep:
The flow'rs had shut their eyes—the zephyr light
  Was gone, for it had rock'd the leaves to sleep;
And all the little birds had laid their heads
Under their wings—sleeping in feather beds.

XV.

Lone in her chamber sate the dark-eyed maid,
  By easy stages jaunting thro' her prayers,
But list'ning side-long to a serenade,
  That robb'd the saints a little of their shares:
For Julio underneath the lattice play'd
  His Deh Vieni, and such amorous airs,
Born only underneath Italian skies,
Where every fiddle has a Bridge of Sighs.

XVI.

Sweet was the tune—the words were even sweeter—
  Praising her eyes, her lips, her nose, her hair,
With all the common tropes wherewith in metre
  The hackney poets overcharge their fair.
Her shape was like Diana's but completer;
  Her brow with Grecian Helen's might compare:
Cupid, alas! was cruel Sagittarius,
Julio—the weeping water-man Aquarius.

XVII.

Now, after listing to such laudings rare,
  'Twas very natural indeed to go—
What if she did postpone one little prayer—
  To ask her mirror " if it was not so ?"
'Twas a large mirror, none the worse for wear,
  Reflecting her at once from top to toe:
And there she gazed upon that glossy track,
That show'd her front face tho' it " gave her back."

XVIII.

And long her lovely eyes were held in thrall,
  By that dear page where first the woman reads :
That Julio was no flatt'rer, none at all,
  She told herself—and then she told her beads ;
Meanwhile, the nerves insensibly let fall
  Two curtains fairer than the lily breeds ;
For Sleep had crept and kiss'd her unawares,
Just at the half-way milestone of her prayers.

XIX.

Then like a drooping rose so bended she,
  Till her bow'd head upon her hand reposed ;
But still she plainly saw, or seem'd to see,
  That fair reflection, tho' her eyes were closed,
A beauty bright as it was wont to be,
  A portrait Fancy painted while she dozed :
'Tis very natural, some people say,
To dream of what we dwell on in the day.

XX.

Still shone her face—yet not, alas ! the same,
  But 'gan some dreary touches to assume,
And sadder thoughts, with sadder changes came—
  Her eyes resign'd their light, her lips their bloom,

Her teeth fell out, her tresses did the same,
   Her cheeks were tinged with bile, her eyes with rheum:
There was a throbbing at her heart within,
For, oh! there was a shooting in her chin.

XXI.

And lo! upon her sad desponding brow,
   The cruel trenches of besieging age,
With seams, but most unseemly, 'gan to show
   Her place was booking for the seventh stage;
And where her raven tresses used to flow,
   Some locks that Time had left her in his rage,
And some mock ringlets, made her forehead shady,
A compound (like our Psalms) of tête and braidy.

XXII.

Then for her shape—alas! how Saturn wrecks,
   And bends, and corkscrews all the frame about,
Doubles the hams, and crooks the straightest necks,
   Draws in the nape, and pushes forth the snout,
Makes backs and stomachs concave or convex:
   Witness those pensioners call'd In and Out,
Who all day watching first and second rater,
Quaintly unbend themselves—but grow no straighter.

XXIII.

So Time with fair Bianca dealt, and made
   Her shape a bow, that once was like an arrow;
His iron hand upon her spine he laid,
   And twisted all awry her " winsome marrow."
In truth it was a change!—she had obey'd
   The holy Pope before her chest grew narrow,
But spectacles and palsy seem'd to make her
Something between a Glassite and a Quaker.

XXIV.

Her grief and gall meanwhile were quite extreme,
 And she had ample reason for her trouble;
For what sad maiden can endure to seem
 Set in for singleness, tho' growing double.
The fancy madden'd her; but now the dream,
 Grown thin by getting bigger, like a bubble,
Burst,—but still left some fragments of its size,
That, like the soapsuds, smarted in her eyes.

XXV.

And here—just here—as she began to heed
 The real world, her clock chimed out its score;
A clock it was of the Venetian breed,
 That cried the hour from one to twenty-four;
The works moreover standing in some need
 Of workmanship, it struck some dozens more;
A warning voice that clench'd Bianca's fears,
Such strokes referring doubtless to her years.

XXVI.

At fifteen chimes she was but half a nun,
 By twenty she had quite renounced the veil;
She thought of Julio just at twenty-one,
 And thirty made her very sad and pale,
To paint that ruin where her charms would run;
 At forty all the maid began to fail,
And thought no higher, as the late dream cross'd her,
Of single blessedness, than single Gloster.

XXVII.

And so Bianca changed;—the next sweet even,
 With Julio in a black Venetian bark,
Row'd slow and stealthily—the hour, eleven,
 Just sounding from the tower of old St. Mark.

She sate with eyes turn'd quietly to heav'n,
　　Perchance rejoicing in the grateful dark
That veil'd her blushing cheek,—for Julio brought her
Of course—to break the ice upon the water.

XXVIII.

But what a puzzle is one's serious mind
　　To open ;—oysters, when the ice is thick,
Are not so difficult and disinclin'd ;
　　And Julio felt the declaration stick
About his throat in a most awful kind ;
　　However, he contrived by bits to pick
His trouble forth,—much like a rotten cork
Grop'd from a long-neck'd bottle with a fork.

XXIX.

But love is still the quickest of all readers ;
　　And Julio spent besides those signs profuse
That English telegraphs and foreign pleaders,
　　In help of language, are so apt to use,
Arms, shoulders, fingers, all were interceders,
　　Nods, shrugs, and bends,—Bianca could not choose
But soften to his suit with more facility,
He told his story with so much agility.

XXX.

" Be thou my park, and I will be thy dear,
　　(So he began at last to speak or quote ;)
Be thou my bark, and I thy gondolier,
　　(For passion takes this figurative note ;)
Be thou my light, and I thy chandelier ;
　　Be thou my dove, and I will be thy cote :
My lily be, and I will be thy river ;
Be thou my life—and I will be thy liver."

XXXI.

This, with more tender logic of the kind,
   He pour'd into her small and shell-like ear,
That timidly against his lips inclin'd;
   Meanwhile her eyes glanc'd on the silver sphere
That even now began to steal behind
   A dewy vapour, which was lingering near,
Wherein the dull moon crept all dim and pale,
Just like a virgin putting on the veil:—

XXXII.

Bidding adieu to all her sparks—the stars,
   That erst had woo'd and worshipp'd in her train,
Saturn and Hesperus, and gallant Mars—
   Never to flirt with heavenly eyes again.
Meanwhile, remindful of the convent bars,
   Bianca did not watch these signs in vain,
But turn'd to Julio at the dark eclipse,
With words, like verbal kisses, on her lips.

XXXIII.

He took the hint full speedily, and, back'd
   By love, and night, and the occasion's meetness,
Bestow'd a something on her cheek that smack'd
   (Tho' quite in silence) of ambrosial sweetness;
That made her think all other kisses lack'd
   Till then, but what she knew not, of completeness:
Being used but sisterly salutes to feel,
Insipid things—like sandwiches of veal.

XXXIV.

He took her hand, and soon she felt him wring
   The pretty fingers all instead of one;
Anon his stealthy arm began to cling
   About her waist that had been clasp'd by none;

Their dear confessions I forbear to sing,
   Since cold description would but be outrun:
For bliss and Irish watches have the pow'r,
   In twenty minutes, to lose half an hour!

IN-AND-OUT PENSIONERS.

M 2

A BALLAD SINGER

Is a town crier for the advertising of lost tunes. Hunger hath made him a wind instrument : his want is vocal, and not he. His voice had gone a-begging before he took it up and applied it to the same trade ; it was too strong to hawk mackarel, but was just soft enough for Robin Adair. His business is to make popular songs unpopular,—he gives the air, like a weather-cock, with many variations. As for a key, he has but one—a latch-key—for all manner of tunes ; and as they are to pass current amongst the lower sorts of people, he makes his notes like a country banker's, as thick as he can. His tones have a copper sound, for he sounds for copper ; and for the musical divisions he hath no regard, but sings on, like a kettle, without taking any heed of the bars. Before beginning he clears his pipe with gin ; and he is always hoarse from the thorough draft in his throat. He hath but one shake, and that is in winter. His voice sounds flat, from flatulence ; and he fetches breath, like a drowning kitten, whenever he can. Notwithstanding all this his music gains ground, for it walks with him from end to end of the street.

He is your only performer that requires not many entreaties for a song ; for he will chaunt, without asking, to a street cur or a parish post. His only backwardness is to a stave after dinner, seeing that he never dines; for he sings for bread, and though corn has ears, sings very commonly in vain. As for his country, he is an Englishman, that by his birthright may sing whether he can or not. To conclude, he is reckoned passable in the city, but is not so good off the stones.

PANDEANS.

MARY'S GHOST.

A PATHETIC BALLAD.

"GIN A BODY MEET A BODY"

I.

'TWAS in the middle of the night,
To sleep young William tried,
When Mary's ghost came stealing in,
And stood at his bed-side.

II.

O William dear! O William dear!
  My rest eternal ceases;
Alas! my everlasting peace
  Is broken into pieces.

III.

I thought the last of all my cares
  Would end with my last minute;
But tho' I went to my long home,
  I didn't stay long in it.

IV.

The body-snatchers they have come,
  And made a snatch at me;
It's very hard them kind of men
  Won't let a body be!

V.

You thought that I was buried deep,
  Quite decent like and chary,
But from her grave in Mary-bone
  They've come and bon'd your Mary.

VI.

The arm that us'd to take your arm
  Is took to Dr. Vyse;
And both my legs are gone to walk
  The hospital at Guy's.

VII.

I vow'd that you should have my hand,
  But fate gives us denial;
You'll find it there, at Doctor Bell's,
  In spirits and a phial.

VIII.

As for my feet, the little feet
    You used to call so pretty,
There's one, I know, in Bedford Row,
    The t'other's in the city.

IX.

I can't tell where my head is gone,
    But Doctor Carpue can:
As for my trunk, it's all pack'd up
    To go by Pickford's van.

X.

I wish you'd go to Mr. P.
    And save me such a ride;
I don't half like the outside place,
    They've took for my inside.

XI.

The cock it crows—I must be gone!
    My William, we must part!
But I'll be your's in death, altho'
    Sir Astley has my heart.

XII.

Don't go to weep upon my grave,
    And think that there I be;
They haven't left an atom there
    Of my anatomie.

THE PROGRESS OF ART.

INFANT GENIUS.

— ✦ —

I.

O HAPPY time! Art's early days!
When o'er each deed, with sweet self-praise,
     Narcissus-like I hung!
When great Rembrandt but little seem'd,
And such Old Masters all were deem'd
     As nothing to the young!

II.

Some scratchy strokes—abrupt and few,
So easily and swift I drew,
　　Suffic'd for my design;
My sketchy, superficial hand,
Drew solids at a dash—and spann'd
　　A surface with a line.

III.

Not long my eye was thus content,
But grew more critical—my bent
　　Essay'd a higher walk;
I copied leaden eyes in lead—
Rheumatic hands in white and red,
　　And gouty feet—in chalk.

IV.

Anon my studious art for days
Kept making faces—happy phrase,
　　For faces such as mine!
Accomplish'd in the details then,
I left the minor parts of men,
　　And drew the form divine.

V.

Old Gods and Heroes—Trojan—Greek,
Figures—long after the antique,
　　Great Ajax justly fear'd;
Hectors, of whom at night I dreamt,
And Nestor, fring'd enough to tempt
　　Bird-nesters to his beard.

VI.

A Bacchus, leering on a bowl,
A Pallas, that out-star'd her owl,
    A Vulcan—very lame ;
A Dian stuck about with stars,
With my right hand I murder'd Mars—
    (One Williams did the same.)

VII.

But tir'd of this dry work at last,
Crayon and chalk aside I cast,
    And gave my brush a drink !
Dipping—" as when a painter dips
In gloom of earthquake and eclipse,"—
    That is—in Indian ink.

VIII.

Oh then, what black Mont Blancs arose,
Crested with soot, and not with snows :
    What clouds of dingy hue !
In spite of what the bard has penn'd,
I fear the distance did not " lend
    Enchantment to the view."

IX.

Not Radclyffe's brush did e'er design
Black Forests, half so black as mine,
    Or lakes so like a pall ;
The Chinese cake dispers'd a ray
Of darkness, like the light of Day
    And Martin over all.

X.

Yet urchin pride sustain'd me still,
I gaz'd on all with right good will,
    And spread the dingy tint;
"No holy Luke help'd me to paint,
The devil surely, not a Saint,
    Had any finger in't!"

XI.

But colours came!—like morning light,
With gorgeous hues displacing night,
    Or Spring's enliven'd scene:
At once the sable shades withdrew;
My skies got very, very blue;
    My trees extremely green.

XII.

And wash'd by my cosmetic brush,
How Beauty's cheek began to blush;
    With lock of auburn stain—
(Not Goldsmith's Auburn)—nut-brown hair,
That made her loveliest of the fair;
    Not "loveliest of the plain!"

XIII.

Her lips were of vermilion hue;
Love in her eyes, and Prussian blue,
    Set all my heart in flame!
A young Pygmalion, I ador'd
The maids I made—but time was stor'd
    With evil—and it came!

XIV.

Perspective dawn'd—and soon I saw
My houses stand against its law ;
    And "keeping" all unkept !
My beauties were no longer things
For love and fond imaginings ;
    But horrors to be wept !

XV.

Ah ! why did knowledge ope my eyes ?
Why did I get more artist-wise ?
    It only serves to hint,
What grave defects and wants are mine ;
That I'm no Hilton in design—
    In nature no Dewint !

XVI.

Thrice happy time !—Art's early days !
When o'er each deed, with sweet self-praise,
    Narcissus-like I hung !
When great Rembrandt but little seem'd,
And such Old Masters all were deem'd
    As nothing to the young !

A SCHOOL FOR ADULTS.

"LETTER LATE THAN NEVER."

Servant.	How well you saw Your father to school to-day, knowing how apt He is to play the truant.
Son.	But is he not Yet gone to school?
Servant.	Stand by, and you shall see.

Enter three Old Men with satchels, singing.

All Three.	Domine, Domine, duster, Three knaves in a cluster.
Son.	O this is gallant pastime. Nay, come on ; Is this your school ? was that your lesson, ha?

1st Old Man.	Pray, now, good son, indeed, indeed—
Son.	Indeed
	You shall to school. Away with him! and take
	Their wagships with him, the whole cluster of them.
2d Old Man.	You shan't send us, now, so you shan't—
3d Old Man.	We be none of your father, so we be'nt.—
Son.	Away with 'em, I say; and tell their school-mistress
	What truants they are, and bid her pay 'em soundly.
All Three.	Oh! oh! oh!
Lady.	Alas! will nobody beg pardon for
	The poo old boys?
Traveller.	Do men of such fair years here go to school?
Native.	They would die dunces else.
	These were great scholars in their youth; but when
	Age grows upon men here, their learning wastes,
	And so decays, that, if they live until
	Threescore, their sons send 'em to school again;
	They'd die as speechless else as new-born children.
Traveller.	'Tis a wise nation, and the piety
	Of the young men most rare and commendable:
	Yet give me, as a stranger, leave to beg
	Their liberty this day.
Son.	'Tis granted.
	Hold up your heads; and thank the gentleman,
	Like scholars, with your heels now.
All Three.	Gratias! Gratias! Gratias! [*Exeunt Singing.*]

"THE ANTIPODES,"—*By R. Brome.*

AMONGST the foundations for the promotion of National Education, I had heard of Schools for Adults; but I doubted of their existence. They were, I thought, merely the fancies of old dramatists, such as that scene just quoted; or the suggestions of philanthropists—the theoretical buildings of modern philosophers—benevolent prospectuses drawn up by warm-hearted enthusiasts, but of schemes never to be realized. They were probably only the bubble projections of a junto of interested pedagogues, not content with the entrance monies of the rising generation, but aiming to exact a premium from the unlettered gray-

beard.   The age, I argued, was not ripe for such
institutions, in spite of the spread of intelligence, and
the vast power of knowledge insisted on by the public
journalist.   I could not conceive a set of men, or
gentlemen, of mature years, if not aged, entering
themselves as members of preparatory schools, and
petty seminaries, in defiance of shame, humiliation,
and the contumely of a literary age.   It seemed too
whimsical to contemplate fathers, and venerable grand-
fathers, emulating the infant generation, and seeking
for instruction in the rudiments.   My imagination
refused to picture the hoary abecedarian,

> ' With satchel on his back, and shining morning face,
>   Creeping, like snail, unwillingly to school."

Fancy grew restive at a patriarchal ignoramus with a
fool's-cap, and a rod thrust down his bosom ; at a
palsied truant dodging the palmy inflictions of the
cane ; or a silver-headed dunce horsed on a pair of
rheumatic shoulders for a paralytic flagellation.   The
picture notwithstanding is realized !   Elderly people
seem to have considered that they will be as awkwardly
situated in the other world, as here, without their
alphabet,—and Schools for Grown Persons to learn to
read, are no more Utopian than New Harmony.   The
following letter from an old gentleman, whose education had been neglected, confirms me in the fact.   It
is copied, verbatim and literatim, from the original,
which fell into my hands by accident.

Deer Brother,   *Black Heath, November*, 1827.

        My honnerd Parents being Both desist
I feal my deuty to give you Sum Acount of the Prog-
gress I have maid in my studdys since last Vocation.

You will be gratefied to hear I am at the Hed of my
Class and Tom Hodges is at its Bottom, tho He was
Seventy last Burth Day and I am onely going on for
Three Skore. I have begun Gografy and do exsizes
on the Globs. In figgers I am all most out the fore
Simples and going into Compounds next weak. In
the mean time hop you will aprove my Hand riting as
well as my Speling witch I have took grate panes with
as you desird. As for the French Tung Mr. Legender
says I shall soon get the pronounciation as well as a
Parishiner but the Master thinks its not advisible to
begin Lattin at my advanced ears.

With respecks to my Pearsonal comfits I am verry
happy and midling Well xcept the old Cumplant in
my To—but the Master is so kind as to let me have a
Cushin for my feat. If their is any thing to cumplane
of its the Vittles. Our Cook dont understand Maid
dishe. Her Currys is xcrabble. Tom Hodges Foot
Man brings him Evry Day soop from Birches. I wish
you providid me the same. On the hole I wish on
menny Acounts I was a Day border partickly as
Barlow sleeps in our Room and coffs all nite long.
His brother's Ashmy is wus then his. He has took
lately to snuff and I have wishes to do the like. Its
very dull after Supper since Mr. Grierson took away
the fellers Pips, and forbid smocking, and allmost
raized a Riot on that hed, and some of the Boys was
to have Been horst for it. I am happy (to) say I
have never been floged as yet and onely Caind once and
that was for damming at the Cooks chops becous they
was so overdun, but there was to have been fore Wiped
yeaster day for Playing Wist in skool hours, but was
Begd off on acount of their Lumbargo.

I am sorry to say Ponder has had another Stroak of

N

the perrylaticks and has no Use of his Lims.   He is
Parrs fag—and Parr has got the Roomytix bysides
very bad but luckly its onely stiffind one Arm so he
has still Hops to get the Star for Heliocution.   Poor
Dick Combs eye site has quite gone or he would have
a good chance for the Silvur Pen.

Mundy was one of the Fellers Burths Days and
we was to have a hole Hollday but he dyed sudnly over
nite of the appoplxy and disappinted us verry much.
Two moor was fetcht home last Weak so that we are
getting very thin partickly when we go out Wauking,
witch is seldom more than three at a time, their is
allways so menny in the nusry.   I forgot to say Gar-
rat run off a mouth ago he got verry Homesick ever
since his Granchilderen cum to sea him at skool,—
Mr. Grierson has expeld him for running away.

On Tuesday a new Schollard cum.   He is a very old
crusty Chap and not much lick'd for that resin by the
rest of the Boys, whom all Teas him, and call him Phig
because he is a retired Grosser.   Mr. Grierson declind
another New Boy because he hadn't had the Mizzles.
I have red Gays Febbles and the other books You
were so kind to send me—and would be glad of moor
partickly the Gentlemans with a Welsh Whig and a
Worming Pan when you foreward my Closebox with my
clean Lining like wise sum moor Fleasy Hoshery for
my legs and the Cardmums I rit for with the French
Grammer &c.   Also weather I am to Dance next
quarter.   The Gimnystacks is being interdeuced into
our Skool but is so Voilent no one follows them but
Old Parr and He cant get up his Pole.

I have no more to rite but hop this letter will
find you as Well as me; Mr. Grierson is in Morning
for Mr. Linly Murry of whose loss you have herd of

—xcept which he is in Quite good Helth and desires
his Respective Complements with witch I remane

Your deutiful and

loving Brother

***** ******

S.P.   Barlow and Phigg have just had a fite in the
Yard about calling names and Phigg has pegged
Barlows tooth out But it was loose before.   Mr. G.
dont allow Puglism, if he nose it among the Boys, as at
their Times of lifes it might be fatle partickly from
puling their Coats of in the open Are.

Our new Husher his cum and is verry well Red in
his Mother's tung, witch is the mane thing with
Beginers but We wish the Frentch Master was changed
on Acount of his Pollyticks and Religun.   Brassbrige
and him is always Squabling about Bonnyparty and
the Pop of Room.   Has for Barlow we cant tell
weather He is Wig or Tory for he cant express his
Sentymints for Colling.

A LEGEND OF NAVARRE.

THE SPARE BED.

I.

'Twas in the reign of Lewis, call'd the Great,
  As one may read on his triumphal arches,
The thing befel I'm going to relate,
  In course of one of those "pomposo" marches
He lov'd to make, like any gorgeous Persian,
Partly for war, and partly for diversion.

II.

Some wag had put it in the royal brain
　To drop a visit at an old chateau,
Quite unexpected, with his courtly train;
　The monarch lik'd it,—but it happened so,
That Death had got before them by a post,
And they were "reckoning without their *host*,"

III.

Who died exactly as a child should die,
　Without one groan or a convulsive breath,
Closing without one pang his quiet eye,
　Sliding composedly from sleep—to death;
A corpse so placid ne'er adorn'd a bed,
He seem'd not quite—but only rather dead.

IV.

All night the widow'd Baroness contriv'd
　To shed a widow's tears; but on the morrow
Some news of such unusual sort arriv'd,
　There came strange alteration in her sorrow;
From mouth to mouth it pass'd, one common humming
Throughout the house—the King! the King is coming!

V.

The Baroness, with all her soul and heart,
　A loyal woman, (now called ultra royal,)
Soon thrust all funeral concerns apart,
　And only thought about a banquet-royal;
In short, by aid of earnest preparation,
The visit quite dismiss'd the visitation.

VI.

And, spite of all her grief for the ex-mate,
  There was a secret hope she could not smother,
That some one, early, might replace "the late "—
  It was too soon to think about another ;
Yet let her minutes of despair be reckon'd
Against her hope, which was but for *a second*.

VII.

She almost thought that being thus bereft
  Just then, was one of time's propitious touches ;
A thread in such a nick so nick'd, it left
  Free opportunity to be a duchess ;
Thus all her care was only to look pleasant,
But as for tears—she dropp'd them—for the present.

VIII.

Her household, as good servants ought to try,
  Look'd like their lady—any thing but sad,
And giggled even that they might not cry,
  To damp fine company ; in truth they had
No time to mourn, thro' choking turkeys' throttles,
Scouring old laces, and reviewing bottles.

IX.

Oh what a hubbub for the house of woe !
  All, resolute to one irresolution,
Kept tearing, swearing, plunging to and fro,
  Just like another French mob-revolution.
There lay the corpse that could not stir a muscle,
But all the rest seem'd Chaos in a bustle.

X.

The Monarch came: oh! who could ever guess
   The Baroness had been so late a weeper!
The kingly grace and more than graciousness,
   Buried the poor defunct some fathoms deeper,—
Could he have had a glance—alas, poor Being!
Seeing would certainly have led to *D*—ing.

XI.

For casting round about her eyes to find
   Some one to whom her chattels to endorse,
The comfortable dame at last inclin'd
   To choose the cheerful Master of the Horse;
He was so gay,—so tender,—the complete
Nice man,—the sweetest of the monarch's suite.

XII.

He saw at once and enter'd in the lists—
   Glance unto glance made amorous replies;
They talk'd together like two egotists,
   In conversation all made up of *eyes:*
No couple ever got so right consort-ish
Within two hours—a courtship rather shortish.

XIII.

At last, some sleepy, some by wine opprest,
   The courtly company began " nid noddin ; "
The King first sought his chamber, and the rest
   Instanter followed by the course he trod in.
I shall not please the scandalous by showing
The order, or disorder of their going.

XIV.

The old Chateau, before that night, had never
   Held half so many underneath its roof;
It task'd the Baroness's best endeavour,
   And put her best contrivance to the proof,
To give them chambers up and down the stairs,
In twos and threes, by singles, and by pairs.

XV.

She had just lodging for the whole—yet barely;
   And some, that were both broad of back and tall,
Lay on spare beds that served them very sparely;
   However, there were beds enough for all;
But living bodies occupied so many,
She could not let the dead one take up any!

XVI.

The act was, certainly, not over decent:
   Some small respect, e'en after death, she ow'd him,
Considering his death had been so recent;
   However, by command, her servants stow'd him,
(I am asham'd to think how he was slubber'd,)
Stuck bolt upright within a corner cupboard!

XVII.

And there he slept as soundly as a post,
   With no more pillow than an oaken shelf;
Just like a kind accommodating host,
   Taking all inconvenience on himself;
None else slept in that room, except a stranger,
A decent man, a sort of Forest Ranger.

XVIII.

Who, whether he had gone too soon to bed,
  Or dreamt himself into an appetite,
Howbeit, he took a longing to be fed,
  About the hungry middle of the night ;
So getting forth, he sought some scrap to eat,
Hopeful of some stray pasty, or cold meat.

XIX.

The casual glances of the midnight moon,
  Bright'ning some antique ornaments of brass,
Guided his gropings to that corner soon,
  Just where it stood, the coffin-safe, alas !
He tried the door—then shook it—and in course
Of time it opened to a little force.

XX.

He put one hand in, and began to grope ;
  The place was very deep and quite as dark as
The middle night ;—when lo ! beyond his hope,
  He felt a something cold, in fact, the carcase ;
Right overjoy'd, he laugh'd, and blest his luck
At finding, as he thought, this haunch of buck !

XXI.

Then striding back for his couteau de chasse,
  Determin'd on a little midnight lunching,
He came again and prob'd about the mass,
  As if to find the fattest bit for munching ;
Not meaning wastefully to cut it all up,
But only to abstract a little collop.

XXII.

But just as he had struck one greedy stroke,
  His hand fell down quite powerless and weak ;
For when he cut the haunch it plainly spoke
  As haunch of ven'son never ought to speak ;
No wonder that his hand could go no further—
Whose could ?—to carve cold meat that bellow'd,
    " murther ! "

XXIII.

Down came the Body with a bounce, and down
  The Ranger sprang, a staircase at a spring,
And bawl'd enough to waken up a town ;
  Some thought that *they* were murder'd, some, the King,
And, like Macduff, did nothing for a season,
But stand upon the spot and bellow, " Treason ! "

XXIV.

A hundred nightcaps gather'd in a mob,
  Torches drew torches, swords brought swords together,
It seem'd so dark and perilous a job ;
  The Baroness came trembling like a feather
Just in the rear, as pallid as a corse,
Leaning against the Master of the Horse.

XXV.

A dozen of the bravest up the stair,
  Well lighted and well watch'd, began to clamber ;
They sought the door—they found it—they were there,
  A dozen heads went poking in the chamber ;
And lo ! with one hand planted on his hurt,
There stood the Body bleeding thro his shirt,—

XXVI.

No passive corse—but like a duellist
   Just smarting from a scratch—in fierce position,
One hand advanc'd, and ready to resist;
   In fact, the Baron doff'd the apparition,
Swearing those oaths the French delight in most,
And for the second time "gave up the ghost!"

XXVII.

A living miracle!—for why?—the knife
   That cuts so many off from grave gray hairs,
Had only carv'd him kindly into life:
   How soon it chang'd the posture of affairs!
The difference one person more or less
Will make in families, is past all guess.

XXVIII.

There stood the Baroness—no widow yet:
   Here stood the Baron—"in the body" still:
There stood the Horses' Master in a pet,
   Choking with disappointment's bitter pill,
To see the hope of his reversion fail,
Like that of riding on a donkey's tail.

XXIX.

The Baron liv'd—'twas nothing but a trance:
   The lady died—'twas nothing but a death:
The cupboard-cut serv'd only to enhance
   This postscript to the old Baronial breath:—
He soon forgave, for the revival's sake,
A little *chop* intended for a *steak!*

THE DEMON-SHIP.

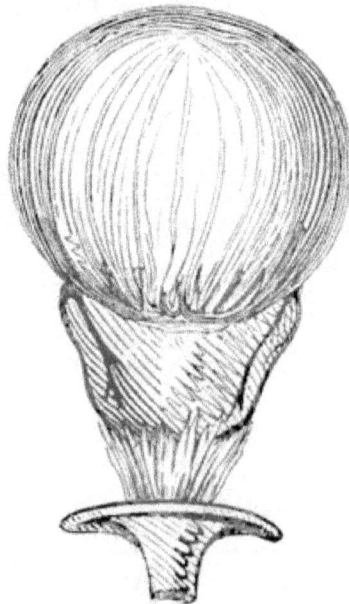

THE FLYING DUTCHMAN.

STORIES of storm-ships and haunted vessels, of spectre-shallops, and supernatural Dutch doggers, are common to many countries, and are well attested both in poetry and prose. The adventures of Solway sailors, with Mahound, in his bottomless barges, and the careerings of the phantom-ship up and down the Hudson, have hundreds of asserters besides Messrs. Cunningham and Crayon; and to doubt their authenticity may seem like an imitation of the desperate

sailing of the haunted vessels themselves against wind
and tide. I cannot help fancying, however, that
Richard Faulder was but one of those tavern-dreamers
recorded by old Heywood, who conceived

"The room wherein they quaff'd to be a pinnace."

And as for the Flying Dutchman, my notion is very
different from the popular conception of that apparition, as I have ventured to show by the opposite
design. The spectre-ship, bound to Dead-Man's Isle,
is almost as awful a craft as the skeleton-bark of the
Ancient Mariner; but they are both fictions, and
have not the advantage of being realities, like the
dreary vessel with its dreary crew in the following
story, which records an adventure that befel even
unto myself.

'Twas off the Wash—the sun went down—the sea
    look'd black and grim,
For stormy clouds, with murky fleece, were mustering
    at the brim ;
Titanic shades! enormous gloom!—as if the solid
    night
Of Erebus rose suddenly to seize upon the light !
It was a time for mariners to bear a wary eye,
With such a dark conspiracy between the sea and sky!

Down went my helm—close reef'd—the tack held
    freely in my hand—
With ballast snug—I put about, and scudded for the
    land.
Loud hiss'd the sea beneath her lee—my little boat
    flew fast,

But faster still the rushing storm came borne upon
the blast.

Lord! what a roaring hurricane beset the straining
sail!

What furious sleet, with level drift, and fierce assaults
of hail!

What darksome caverns yawn'd before! what jagged
steeps behind!

Like battle-steeds, with foamy manes, wild tossing in
the wind.

Each after each sank down astern, exhausted in the
chase,

But where it sank another rose and gallop'd in its
place;

As black as night—they turned to white, and cast
against the cloud

A snowy sheet, as if each surge upturn'd a sailor's
shroud:—

Still flew my boat; alas! alas! her course was nearly
run!

Behold you fatal billow rise—ten billows heap'd in
one!

With fearful speed the dreary mass came rolling,
rolling, fast,

As if the scooping sea contain'd one only wave at
last!

Still on it came, with horrid roar, a swift pursuing
grave;

It seem'd as though some cloud had turn'd its hugeness to a wave!

Its briny sleet began to beat beforehand in my face—

I felt the rearward keel begin to climb its swelling
base!

I saw its alpine hoary head impending over mine!

Another pulse—and down it rush'd—an avalanche of
    brine!
Brief pause had I, on God to cry, or think of wife and
    home;
The waters clos'd—and when I shriek'd, I shriek'd
    below the foam!
Beyond that rush I have no hint of any after deed—
For I was tossing on the waste, as senseless as a
    weed.

      *   *   *   *   *

" Where am I? in the breathing world, or in the
    world of death? "
With sharp and sudden pang I drew another birth of
    breath;
My eyes drank in a doubtful light, my ears a doubtful
    sound—
And was that ship a *real* ship whose tackle seem'd
    around?
A moon, as if the earthly moon, was shining up aloft;
But were those beams the very beams that I had seen
    so oft?
A face, that mock'd the human face, before me watch'd
    alone;
But were those eyes the eyes of man that look'd against
    my own?

Oh! never may the moon again disclose me such a sight
As met my gaze, when first I look'd, on that accursed
    night!
I've seen a thousand horrid shapes begot of fierce
    extremes
Of fever; and most frightful things have haunted in
    my dreams—

Hyenas—cats—blood-loving bats—and apes with hate-
  ful stare—
Pernicious snakes, and shaggy bulls—the lion, and
  she-bear—
Strong enemies, with Judas looks, of treachery and
  spite—
Detested features, hardly dimm'd and banish'd by the
  light!
Pale-sheeted ghosts, with gory locks, upstarting from
  their tombs—
All phantasies and images that flit in midnight
  glooms—
Hags, goblins, demons, lemures, have made me all
  aghast,—
But nothing like that GRIMLY ONE who stood beside
  the mast!

His cheek was black—his brow was black—his eyes
  and hair as dark :
His hand was black, and where it touch'd, it left a
  sable mark ;
His throat was black, his vest the same, and when I
  look'd beneath,
His breast was black—all, all was black, except his
  grinning teeth.
His sooty crew were like 'in hue, as black as Afric
  slaves !
Oh, horror ! e'en the ship was black that plough'd the
  inky waves !

" Alas ! " I cried, " for love of truth and blessed
  mercy's sake,
Where am I ? in what dreadful ship ? upon what
  dreadful lake ?

What shape is that, so very grim, and black as any
    coal?
It is Mahound, the Evil One, and he has gain'd my
    soul!
Oh, mother dear! my tender nurse! dear meadows
    that beguil'd
My happy days, when I was yet a little sinless child,—
My mother dear—my native fields, I never more shall
    see:
I'm sailing in the Devil's Ship, upon the Devil's Sea!"

Loud laugh'd that SABLE MARINER, and loudly in
    return
His sooty crew sent forth a laugh that rang from stem
    to stern—
A dozen pair of grimly cheeks were crumpled on the
    nonce—
As many sets of grinning teeth came shining out at
    once:
A dozen gloomy shapes at once enjoy'd the merry fit,
With shriek and yell, and oaths as well, like Demons
    of the Pit.
They crow'd their fill, and then the Chief made answer
    for the whole;—
"Our skins," said he, "are black ye see, because we
    carry coal;
You'll find your mother sure enough, and see your
    native fields—
For this here ship has pick'd you up—the Mary Ann
    of Shields!"

SALLY HOLT, AND THE DEATH OF JOHN HAYLOFT.

Four times in the year—twice at the season of the
half-yearly dividends, and twice at the intermediate
quarters, to make her slender investments—there calls
at my Aunt Shakerly's, a very plain, very demure
maiden, about forty, and makes her way downward to
the kitchen, or upward to my cousin's chamber, as
may happen. Her coming is not to do chair-work, or
needle-work—to tell fortunes—to beg, steal, or borrow.
She does not come for old clothes, or for new. Her
simple errand is love—pure, strong, disinterested,
enduring love, passing the love of women—at least for
women.

It is not often servitude begets much kindliness
between the two relations; hers, however, grew from
that ungenial soil. For the whole family of the
Shakerlies she has a strong feudal attachment, but her
particular regard dwells with Charlotte, the latest born
of the clan. *Her* she doats upon—*her* she fondles—
and takes upon her longing, loving lap.

O let not the oblivious attentions of the worthy
Dominie Sampson, to the tall boy Bertram, be called
an unnatural working! I have seen my cousin, a
good feeder, and well grown into womanhood, sitting
—two good heads taller than her dry-nurse—on the
knees of the simple-hearted Sally Holt! I have seen

the huge presentation orange, unlapp'd from the homely speckled kerchief, and thrust with importunate tenderness into the bashful *marriageable* hand.

My cousin's heart is not so artificially composed, as to let her scorn this humble affection, though she is puzzled sometimes with what kind of look to receive these honest but awkward endearments. I have seen her face quivering with half a laugh.

It is one of Sally's staple hopes that, some day or other, when Miss Charlotte keeps house, she will live with her as a servant; and this expectation makes her particular and earnest to a fault in her enquiries about sweethearts, and offers, and the matrimonial chances: questions which I have seen my cousin listen to with half a cry.

Perhaps Sally looks upon this confidence as her right, in return for those secrets which, by joint force of ignorance and affection, she could not help reposing in the bosom of her foster-mistress. Nature, unkind to her, as to Dogberry, denied to her that knowledge of reading and writing which comes to some by instinct. A strong principle of religion made it a darling point with her to learn to read, that she might study in her bible: but in spite of all the help of my cousin, and as ardent a desire for learning as ever dwelt in scholar, poor Sally never mastered beyond A-B-ab. Her mind, simple as her heart, was unequal to any more difficult combinations. Writing was worse to her than conjuring. My cousin was her amanuensis: and from the vague, unaccountable mistrust of ignorance, the inditer took the pains always to compare the verbal message with the transcript, by counting the number of the words.

I would give up all the tender epistles of Mrs.

Arthur Brooke, to have read one of Sally's epistles;
but they were amatory, and therefore kept sacred:
for plain as she was, Sally Holt had a lover.

There is an unpretending plainness in some faces
that has its charm—an unaffected ugliness, a thousand
times more bewitching than those would-be pretty
looks that neither satisfy the critical sense, nor leave
the matter of beauty at once to the imagination. We
like better to make a new face than to mend an old
one. Sally had not one good feature, except those
which John Hayloft made for her in his dreams; and
to judge from one token, her partial fancy was equally
answerable for his charms. One precious lock—no,
not a lock, but rather a remnant of very short, very
coarse, very yellow hair, the clippings of a military
crop, for John was a corporal—stood the foremost
item amongst her treasures. To her they were curls,
golden, Hyperion, and cherished long after the parent-
head was laid low, with many more, on the bloody
plain of Salamanca.

I remember vividly at this moment the ecstasy of
her grief at the receipt of the fatal news. She was
standing near the dresser with a dish, just cleaned, in
her dexter hand. Ninety-nine women in a hundred
would have dropped the dish. Many would have
flung themselves after it on the floor; but Sally put
it up, orderly, on the shelf. The fall of John Hayloft
could not induce the fall of the crockery. She felt the
blow notwithstanding; and as soon as she had emptied
her hands, began to give way to her emotions in her
own manner. Affliction vents itself in various modes,
with different temperaments: some rage, others
compose themselves like monuments. Some weep,
some sleep, some prose about death, and others poetise

on it. Many take to a bottle, or to a rope. Some go to Margate, or Bath.

Sally did nothing of these kinds. She neither snivelled, travelled, sickened, maddened, nor ranted, nor canted, nor hung, nor fuddled herself—*she only rocked herself upon the kitchen chair ! !*

The action was not adequate to her relief. She got up—took a fresh chair—then another—and another— and another,—till she had rocked on all the chairs in the kitchen.

The thing was tickling to both sympathies. It was pathetical to behold her grief, but ludicrous that she knew no better how to grieve.

An American might have thought that she was in the act of enjoyment, but for an intermitting O dear! O dear! Passion could not wring more from her in the way of exclamation than the tooth-ache. Her lamentations were always the same, even in tone. By and bye she pulled out the hair—the cropped, yellow, stunted, scrubby hair; then she fell to rocking —then O dear! O dear!—and then Da Capo.

It was an odd sort of elegy, and yet, simple as it was, I thought it worth a thousand of Lord Littleton's!

"Heyday, Sally! what is the matter?" was a very natural inquiry from my Aunt, when she came down into the kitchen; and if she did not make it with her tongue, at least it was asked very intelligibly by her eyes. Now Sally had but one way of addressing her mistress, and she used it here. It was the same with which she would have asked for a holiday, except that the waters stood in her eyes.

"If you please, Ma'am," said she, rising up from her chair, and dropping her old curtsey, " if you please, Ma'am, it's John Hayloft is dead:" and then she began rocking again, as if grief was a baby that wanted jogging to sleep.

My Aunt was posed. She would fain have comforted the mourner, but her mode of grieving was so out of the common way, that she did not know how to begin. To the violent she might have brought soothing; to the desponding, texts of patience and resignation; to the hysterical, sal volatile; she might have asked the sentimental for the story of her woes. A good scolding is useful with some sluggish griefs: —in some cases a cordial. In others—a job.

If Sally had only screamed, or bellowed, or fainted, or gone stupified, or raved, or said a collect, or moped about, it would have been easy to deal with her. But with a woman that only rocked on her chair——

What the devil could my Aunt do ?—

Why, nothing :—and she did it as well as she could.

A SPOONEY.

A TRUE STORY.

A SHOOTING TOOTH.

OF all our pains, since man was curst,
I mean of body, not the mental,
To name the worst, among the worst,
The dental sure is transcendental;
Some bit of masticating bone,
That ought to help to clear a shelf,
But let its proper work alone,
And only seems to gnaw itself;
In fact, of any grave attack

On victual there is little danger,
'Tis so like coming to the *rack*,
As well as going to the manger.

Old Hunks—it seem'd a fit retort
Of justice on his grinding ways—
Possess'd a grinder of the sort,
That troubled all his latter days.
The best of friends fall out, and so
His teeth had done some years ago,
Save some old stumps with ragged root,
And they took turn about to shoot;
If he drank any chilly liquor,
They made it quite a point to throb;
But if he warm'd it on the hob,
Why then they only twitch'd the quicker.

One tooth—I wonder such a tooth
Had never kill'd him in his youth—
One tooth he had with many fangs,
That shot at once as many pangs,
It had an universal sting;
One touch of that extatic stump
Could jerk his limbs, and make him jump,
Just like a puppet on a string;
And what was worse than all, it had
A way of making others bad.
There is, as many know, a knack,
With certain farming undertakers,
And this same tooth pursued their track,
By adding *achers* still to *achers !*

One way there is, that has been judg'd
A certain cure, but Hunks was loth

To pay the fee, and quite begrudg'd
To lose his tooth and money both ;
In fact, a dentist and the wheel
Of Fortune are a kindred cast,
For after all is drawn, you feel
It's paying for a blank at last ;
So Hunks went on from week to week,
And kept his torment in his cheek ;
Oh ! how it sometimes set him rocking,
With that perpetual gnaw—gnaw—gnaw,
His moans and groans were truly shocking
And loud,—altho' he held his jaw.
Many a tug he gave his gum,
And tooth, but still it would not come,
Tho' tied by string to some firm thing,
He could not draw it, do his best,
By draw'rs, altho' he tried a chest.

At last, but after much debating,
He joined a score of mouths in waiting,
Like his, to have their troubles out.
Sad sight it was to look about
At twenty faces making faces,
With many a rampant trick and antic,
For all were very horrid cases,
And made their owners nearly frantic.
A little wicket now and then
Took one of these unhappy men,
And out again the victim rush'd,
While eyes and mouth together gush'd ;
At last arrived our hero's turn,
Who plunged his hands in both his pockets,
And down he sat, prepared to learn
How teeth are charm'd to quit their sockets.

Those who have felt such operations,
Alone can guess the sort of ache,
When his old tooth began to break
The thread of old associations ;
It touch'd a string in every part,
It had so many tender ties ;
One chord seem'd wrenching at his heart,
And two were tugging at his eyes ;
" Bone of his bone," he felt of course,
As husbands do in such divorce ;
At last the fangs gave way a little,
Hunks gave his head a backward jerk,
And lo ! the cause of all this work,
Went—where it used to send his victual !

The monstrous pain of this proceeding
Had not so numb'd his miser wit,
But in this slip he saw a hit
To save, at least, his purse from bleeding ;
So when the dentist sought his fees,
Quoth Hunks, " Let's finish, if you please."
" How, finish ! why it's out ! "—" Oh ! no—
'Tis you are out, to argue so ;
I'm none of your before-hand tippers,
My tooth is in my head no doubt,
But as you say you pull'd it out,
Of course it's there—between your nippers."
" Zounds ! sir, d'ye think I'd sell the truth
To get a fee ? no, wretch, I scorn it."
But Hunks still ask'd to see the tooth,
And swore by gum ! he had not drawn it.

His end obtain'd, he took his leave,
A secret chuckle in his sleeve ;

The joke was worthy to produce one,
To think, by favour of his wit,
How well a dentist had been bit
By one old stump, and that a loose one!
The thing was worth a laugh, but mirth
Is still the frailest thing on earth:
Alas! how often when a joke
Seems in our sleeve, and safe enough,
There comes some unexpected stroke,
And hangs a weeper on the cuff!

Hunks had not whistled half a mile,
When, planted right against a stile,
There stood his foeman, Mike Mahoney,
A vagrant reaper, Irish-born,
That help'd to reap our miser's corn,
But had not help'd to reap his money,
A fact that Hunks remembered quickly;
His whistle all at once was quell'd,
And when he saw how Michael held
His sickle, he felt rather sickly.

Nine souls in ten, with half his fright,
Would soon have paid the bill at sight,
But misers (let observers watch it)
Will never part with their delight
Till well demanded by a hatchet—
They live hard—and they die to match it.
Thus Hunks prepared for Mike's attacking,
Resolved not yet to pay the debt,
But let him take it out in hacking;
However, Mike began to stickle
In words before he used the sickle;
But mercy was not long attendant:

From words at last he took to blows,
And aim'd a cut at Hunks's nose;
That made it what some folks are not—
A member very independent.

Heaven knows how far this cruel trick
Might still have led, but for a tramper
That came in danger's very nick,
To put Mahoney to the scamper.
But still compassion met a damper;
There lay the sever'd nose, Alas!
Beside the daisies on the grass,
" Wee, crimson-tipt " as well as they,
According to the poet's lay:
And there stood Hunks, no sight for laughter!
Away ran Hodge to get assistance,
With nose in hand, which Hunks ran after,
But somewhat at unusual distance.
In many a little country place
It is a very common case
To have but one residing doctor,
Whose practice rather seems to be
No practice, but a rule of three,
Physician—surgeon—drug-decoctor;
Thus Hunks was forced to go once more
Where he had ta'en his tooth before.
His mere name made the learn'd man hot,—
" What! Hunks again within my door!
" I'll pull his nose;" quoth Hunks, " you cannot."

The doctor look'd and saw the case
Plain as the nose *not* on his face.
" O! hum—ha—yes—I understand."
But then arose a long demur,

For not a finger would he stir
Till he was paid his fee in hand;
That matter settled, there they were,
With Hunks well strapp'd upon his chair.

The opening of a surgeon's job—
His tools, a chestfull or a drawfull—
Are always something very awful,
And give the heart the strangest throb;
But never patient in his funks
Look'd half so like a ghost as Hunks,
Or surgeon half so like a devil
Prepared for some internal revel:
His huge black eye kept rolling, rolling,
Just like a bolus in a box:
His fury seem'd above controlling,
He bellow'd like a hunted ox:
"Now, swindling wretch, I'll show thee how
We treat such cheating knaves as thou;
Oh! sweet is this revenge to sup;
I have thee by the nose—it's now
My turn—and I will turn it up."

Guess how the miser liked the scurvy
And cruel way of venting passion;
The snubbing folks in this new fashion
Seem'd quite to turn him topsy turvy;
He utter'd pray'rs, and groans, and curses.
For things had often gone amiss
And wrong with him before, but this
Would be the worst of all *reverses!*
In fancy he beheld his snout
Turn'd upward like a pitcher's spout;
There was another grievance yet,

And fancy did not fail to show it,
That he must throw a summerset,
Or stand upon his head to blow it.

And was there then no argument
To change the doctor's vile intent,
And move his pity?—yes, in truth,
And that was—paying for the tooth.
" Zounds! pay for such a stump! I'd rather   "
But here the menace went no farther,
For with his other ways of pinching,
Hunks had a miser's love of snuff,
A recollection strong enough
To cause a very serious flinching;
In short he paid and had the feature
Replaced as it was meant by nature;
For tho' by this 'twas cold to handle,
(No corpse's could have felt more horrid,)
And white just like an end of candle,
The doctor deem'd and proved it too,
That noses from the nose will do
As well as noses from the forehead;
So, fix'd by dint of rag and lint,
The part was bandag'd up and muffled.
The chair unfasten'd, Hunks arose,
And shuffled out, for once unshuffled;
And as he went, these words he snuffled—
" Well, this *is* ' paying thro' the nose.' "

THE DECLINE OF MRS. SHAKERLY.

"WHOLESALE—RETAIL—AND FOR EXPORTATION."

Towards the close of her life, my Aunt Shakerly increased rapidly in bulk: she kept adding growth unto her growth,

"Giving a sum of more to that which had too much,"

till the result was worthy of a Smithfield premium.   It was not the triumph, however, of any systematic diet for the promotion of fat,—(except oyster-eating there is no human system of *stall*-feeding,) on the contrary, she lived abstemiously, diluting her food with pickle-acids, and keeping frequent fasts, in order to reduce her compass; but they failed of this desirable effect. Nature had planned an original tendency in her organisation that was not to be overcome :—she would have fattened on sour krout.

My uncle, on the other hand, decreased daily; originally a little man, he became lean, shrunken, wizened. There was a predisposition in his constitution that made him spare, and kept him so:—he would have fallen off even on brewers' grains.

It was the common joke of the neighbourhood to designate my aunt, my uncle, and the infant Shakerly, as " WHOLESALE, RETAIL, and FOR EXPORTATION;" and, in truth, they were not inapt impersonations of that popular inscription,—my aunt a giantess, my uncle a pigmy, and the child being "carried abroad."

Alas! of the three departments, nothing now remains but the Retail portion—my uncle, a penny-worth, a mere sample.

It is upon record, that Dr. Watts, though a puny man in person, took a fancy, towards his latter days, that he was too large to pass through a door: an error which Death shortly corrected by taking him through his own portal. My unhappy aunt, with more show of reason, indulged in a similar delusion; she conceived herself to have grown inconveniently cumbersome for the small village of * * * *, and my uncle, to quiet her, removed to the metropolis. There she lived for some months in comparative ease, till at last an unlucky event recalled all her former inquietude. The Elephant of Mr. Cross, a good feeder, and with a natural tendency to corpulence, throve so well on his rations, that, becoming too huge for his den, he was obliged to be dispatched. My aunt read the account in the newspapers, and the catastrophe with its cause took possession of her mind. She seemed to herself as that Elephant. An intolerable sense of confinement and oppression haunted her by day and in her dreams. First she had a tightness at her chest, then in her limbs, then all over; she felt too big for her chair—then for her bed—then for her room—then for the house! To divert her thought my uncle proposed to go to Paris; but she was too huge for a boat—for a barge—for a packet—for a frigate—for a country—for a continent! "She was too big," she said, "for this world—but she was going to one that is boundless."

Nothing could wean her from this belief: her whole talk was of "cumber-grounds:" of the "burthen of the flesh:" and of "infinity." Sometimes her head wandered, and she would then speak of disposing of the "bulk of her personals."

In the meantime her health decayed slowly, but perceptibly: she was dying, the doctor said, by inches.

Now my uncle was a kind husband, and meant tenderly, though it sounded untender: but when the doctor said that she was dying by inches—

"God forbid!" cried my uncle: "consider what a great big creature she is!"

TIM TURPIN,

A PATHETIC BALLAD.

THE JUDGES OF A-SIZE.

I.

TIM TURPIN he was gravel blind,
  And ne'er had seen the skies:
For Nature, when his head was made,
  Forgot to dot his eyes.

II.

So, like a Christmas pedagogue,
  Poor Tim was forc'd to do—
Look out for pupils, for he had
  A vacancy for two.

III.

There's some have specs to help their sight
    Of objects dim and small :
But Tim had *specks* within his eyes,
    And could not see at all.

IV.

Now Tim he woo'd a servant maid,
    And took her to his arms ;
For he, like Pyramus, had cast
    A wall-eye on her charms.

V.

By day she led him up and down
    Where'er he wish'd to jog,
A happy wife, altho' she led
    The life of any dog.

VI.

But just when Tim had liv'd a month
    In honey with his wife,
A surgeon ope'd his Milton eyes,
    Like oysters, with a knife.

VII.

But when his eyes were open'd thus,
    He wish'd them dark again :
For when he look'd upon his wife,
    He saw her very plain.

VIII.

Her face was bad, her figure worse,
    He couldn't bear to eat :
For she was any thing but like
    A Grace before his meat.

IX.

Now Tim he was a feeling man :
　For when his sight was thick,
It made him feel for every thing—
　But that was with a stick.

X.

So with a cudgel in his hand—
　It was not light or slim—
He knocked at his wife's head until
　It open'd unto him.

XI.

And when the corpse was stiff and cold
　He took his slaughter'd spouse,
And laid her in a heap with all
　The ashes of her house.

XII.

But like a wicked murderer,
　He liv'd in constant fear
From day to day, and so he cut
　His throat from ear to ear.

XIII.

The neighbours fetch'd a doctor in :
　Said he, this wound I dread
Can hardly be sow'd up—his life
　Is hanging on a thread.

XIV.

But when another week was gone,
　He gave him stronger hope—
Instead of hanging on a thread,
　Of hanging on a rope.

XV.

Ah! when he hid his bloody work,
  In ashes round about,
How little he supposed the truth
  Would soon be sifted out.

XVI.

But when the parish dustman came,
  His rubbish to withdraw,
He found more dust within the heap,
  Than he contracted for!

XVII.

A dozen men to try the fact,
  Were sworn that very day;
But tho' they all were jurors, yet
  No conjurors were they.

XVIII.

Said Tim unto those jurymen,
  You need not waste your breath,
For I confess myself at once,
  The author of her death.

XIX.

And, oh! when I reflect upon
  The blood that I have spilt,
Just like a button is my soul,
  Inscrib'd with double *guilt!*

XX.

Then turning round his head again,
  He saw before his eyes,
A great judge, and a little judge,
  The judges of a-size!

XXI.

The great judge took his judgment cap,
   And put it on his head,
And sentenc'd Tim by law to hang,
   Till he was three times dead.

XXII.

So he was tried, and he was hung
   (Fit punishment for such)
On Horsham-drop, and none can say
   It was a drop too much.

JURORS—NOT CON-JURORS.

THE MONKEY-MARTYR.

A FABLE.

BRUTE EMANCIPATION.

"God help thee, said I, but I'll let thee out, cost what it will : so I
turned about the cage to get to the door."—STERNE.

———◆———

'TIS strange, what awkward figures and odd capers
Folks cut, who seek their doctrine from the papers ;
But there are many shallow politicians,
Who take their bias from bewilder'd journals—
      Turn state-physicians,
And make themselves fools'-caps of the diurnals.

One of this kind, not human, but a monkey,
Had read himself at last to this sour creed—
That he was nothing but Oppression's flunkey,
And man a tyrant over all his breed.
   He could not read
Of niggers whipt, or over-trampled weavers,
But he applied their wrongs to his own seed,
And nourish'd thoughts that threw him into fevers.
His very dreams were full of martial beavers,
And drilling Pugs, for liberty pugnacious,
   To sever chains vexatious :
In fact, he thought that all his injur'd line
Should take up pikes in hand, and never drop 'em
Till they had clear'd a road to Freedom's shrine,—
Unless perchance the turn-pike men should stop 'em.

   Full of this rancour,
Pacing one day beside St. Clement Danes,
   It came into his brains
To give a look in at the Crown and Anchor;
Where certain solemn sages of the nation
Were at that moment in deliberation
How to relieve the wide world of its chains,
   Pluck despots down,
   And thereby crown
Whitee- as well as blackee-man-cipation.
Pug heard the speeches with great approbation,
And gaz'd with pride upon the Liberators ;
   To see mere coal-heavers
   Such perfect Bolivars—
Waiters of inns sublim'd to innovators,
And slaters dignified as legislators—
Small publicans demanding (such their high sense
Of liberty) an universal license—

And patten-makers easing Freedom's clogs—
  The whole thing seem'd
  So fine, he deem'd
The smallest demagogues as great as Gogs!

Pug, with some curious notions in his noddle,
Walk'd out at last, and turn'd into the Strand,
  To the left hand,
Conning some portions of the previous twaddle,
And striding with a step that seem'd design'd
To represent the mighty March of Mind,
  Instead of that slow waddle
Of thought, to which our ancestors inclin'd—
No wonder, then, that he should quickly find
He stood in front of that intrusive pile,
  Where Cross keeps many a kind
  Of bird confin'd,
And free-born animal, in durance vile—
A thought that stirr'd up all the monkey-bile!

  The window stood ajar—
  It was not far,
Nor, like Parnassus, very hard to climb—
The hour was verging on the supper-time,
And many a growl was sent through many a bar.
Meanwhile Pug scrambled upward like a tar,
  And soon crept in,
  Unnotic'd in the din
Of tuneless throats, that made the attics ring
With all the harshest notes that they could bring;
  For like the Jews,
  Wild beasts refuse,
In midst of their captivity—to sing.

Lord! how it made him chafe,
Full of his new emancipating zeal,
To look around upon this brute-bastille,
And see the king of creatures in—a safe!
The desert's denizen in one small den,
Swallowing slavery's most bitter pills—
A bear in bars unbearable.   And then
The fretful porcupine, with all its quills
   Imprison'd in a pen!
 A tiger limited to four feet ten;
   And, still worse lot,
   A leopard to one spot!
   An elephant enlarg'd,
   But not discharg'd;
 (It was before the elephant was shot:)
A doleful wanderoo, that wandered not;
An ounce much disproportion'd to his pound.
   Pug's wrath wax'd hot
To gaze upon these captive creatures round;
Whose claws—all scratching—gave him full assurance
They found their durance vile of vile endurance.

He went above—a solitary mounter
Up gloomy stairs—and saw a pensive group
   Of hapless fowls—
   Cranes, vultures, owls,
In fact, it was a sort of Poultry-Compter,
Where feather'd prisoners were doom'd to droop:
Here sat an eagle, forc'd to make a stoop,
Not from the skies, but his impending roof;
   And there aloof,
A pining ostrich, moping in a coop;
With other samples of the bird creation,
All cag'd against their powers and their wills,

And cramp'd in such a space, the longest bills
Were plainly bills of least accommodation.
In truth, it was a very ugly scene
To fall to any liberator's share,
To see those winged fowls, that once had been
Free as the wind, no freer than fix'd air.

  His temper little mended,
Pug from this Bird-cage Walk at last descended
   Unto the lion and the elephant,
   His bosom in a pant
To see all nature's Free List thus suspended,
And beasts depriv'd of what she had intended.
   They could not even prey
   In their own way;
A hardship always reckon'd quite prodigious.
   Thus he revolv'd—
   And soon resolv'd
To give them freedom, civil and religious.

That night there were no country cousins, raw
From Wales, to view the lion and his kin :
The keeper's eyes were fix'd upon a saw ;
The saw was fix'd upon a bullock's shin :
   Meanwhile with stealthy paw,
   Pug hastened to withdraw
The bolt that kept the king of brutes within.
Now, monarch of the forest ! thou shalt win
Precious enfranchisement—thy bolts are undone ;
Thou art no longer a degraded creature,
But loose to roam with liberty and nature ;
And free of all the jungles about London—
All Hampstead's heathy desert lies before thee !
Methinks I see thee bound from Cross's ark,

Full of the native instinct that comes o'er thee,
        And turn a ranger
Of Hounslow Forest, and the Regent's Park—
Thin Rhodes's cows—the mail-coach steeds endanger,
And gobble parish watchman after dark :—
Methinks I see thee, with the early lark,
Stealing to Merlin's cave—(*thy* cave.)—Alas,
That such bright visions should not come to pass!
Alas, for freedom, and for freedom's hero!
        Alas, for liberty of life and limb!
For Pug had only half unbolted Nero,
        When Nero *bolted him !*

PONY-ATOWSKI.

BANDITTI.

— ◆ —

OF all the saints in the Calendar, none has suffered less from the Reformation than St. Cecilia, the great patroness of Music. Lofty and lowly are her votaries —many and magnificent are her holiday festivals— and her common service is performing at all hours of the day. She has not only her regular high-priests and priestesses; but, like the Wesleyans, her itinerants and street-missionaries, to make known her worship in the highways and in the byeways. Nor is the homage confined to the people of one creed;—the Protestant exalts her on his barrel-organ—the Catholic with her tambourine—the wandering Jew with his Pan's-pipe and double-drum. The group on the other side was sketched from a company of these " Strolling Players."

It must be confessed that their service is sometimes of a kind rather to drive angels higher into heaven, than to entice them earthward; and there are certain retired streets—near the Adelphi, for instance—where such half-hourly deductions from the natural quiet of the situation should justly be considered in the rent. Some of the choruses, in truth, are beyond any but a saintly endurance. Conceive a brace of opposition organs, a fife, two hurdy-gurdies, a clarionet, and a quartette of decayed mariners, all clubbing their music in common, on the very principle of Mr. Owen's *New Harmony!*

In the Journal of a recent Traveller through the Papal States, there is an account of an adventure with Neapolitan robbers, that would serve, with very slight alterations, for the description of an encounter with our own banditti.

" To-day, Mrs. Graham and I mounted our horses and rode towards Islington. We had not proceeded far, when we heard sounds as of screaming and groaning, and presently a group of men appeared at a turn of the road, It was too certain that we had fallen in with one of those roving bands. Escape was impossible, as they extended across the road. Their leader was the celebrated Flanigan, notorious for his murder of Fair Ellen, and the Bewildered Maid. One of the fellows advanced close up to Mrs. G., and putting his instrument to her ear, threatened to blow out her brains. We gave them what coppers we had, and were allowed to proceed. We were informed by the country-people, that a gentlewoman and her daughter had been detained by them, near the same spot, and robbed of their hearings, with circumstances of great barbarity ; Flanigan in the meantime, standing by with his pipe in his mouth!

"Innumerable other travellers have been stopped and tortured by these wretches, till they gave up their money : and yet these excesses are winked at by the police. In the meantime, the government does not interfere, in the hope, perhaps, that some day those gangs may be broken up, and separated, by discord amongst themselves."

Sometimes to the eye of fancy these wandering minstrels assume another character, and illustrate Collins's Ode on the Passions, in a way that might edify Miss Macauley. First, Fear, a blind harper, lays his bewildered hand amongst the chords, but recoils back at the sound of an approaching carriage. Anger, with starting eye-balls, blows a rude clash on the bugle-horn ; and Despair, a snipe-faced wight, beguiles his grief with low sullen sounds on the bassoon. Hope, a consumptive Scot, with golden hair and a clarionet, indulges, like the flatterer herself, in a thousand fantastic flourishes beside the tune—with a lingering quaver at the close ; and would quaver longer, but Revenge shakes his matted locks, blows a fresh alarum on his pandeans, and thumps with double heat his double-drum. Dejected Pity at his side, a hunger-bitten urchin, applies to his silver-toned triangle ; whilst Jealousy, sad proof of his distracted state, grinds on, in all sorts of time, at his barrel-organ. With eyes upraised, pale Melancholy sings retired and unheeded at the corner of the street ; and Mirth,—yonder he is, a brisk little Savoyard, jerking away at the hurdy-gurdy, and dancing himself at the same time, to render his jig-tune more jigging.

DEATH'S RAMBLE.

"DUST O!"

One day the dreary old King of Death
  Inclined for some sport with the carnal,
So he tied a pack of darts on his back,
  And quietly stole from his charnel.

His head was bald of flesh and of hair,
  His body was lean and lank,
His joints at each stir made a crack, and the cur
  Took a gnaw, by the way, at his shank.

And what did he do with his deadly darts,
  This goblin of grisly bone ?
He dabbled and spill'd man's blood, and he kill'd
  Like a butcher that kills his own.

The first he slaughter'd it made him laugh,
  (For the man was a coffin-maker,)
To think how the mutes, and men in black suits,
  Would mourn for an undertaker.

Death saw two Quakers sitting at church,
  Quoth he, " we shall not differ."
And he let them alone, like figures of stone
  For he could not make them stiffer.

He saw two duellists going to fight,
  In fear they could not smother ;
And he shot one through at once—for he knew
  They never would shoot each other.

He saw a watchman fast in his box,
  And he gave a snore infernal ;
Said Death, " he may keep his breath, for his sleep
  Can never be more eternal."

He met a coachman driving his coach
  So slow, that his fare grew sick ;
But he let him stray on his tedious way,
  For Death only wars on the *quick*.

Death saw a toll-man taking a toll,
  In the spirit of his fraternity ;
But he knew that sort of man would extort,
  Though summon'd to all eternity.

Q

He found an author writing his life,
    But he let him write no further;
For Death, who strikes whenever he likes,
    Is jealous of all self-murther!

Death saw a patient that pull'd out his purse,
    And a doctor that took the sum;
But he let them be—for he knew that the "fee"
    Was a prelude to "faw" and "fum."

He met a dustman ringing a bell,
    And he gave him a mortal thrust;
For himself, by law, since Adam's flaw,
    Is contractor for all our dust.

He saw a sailor mixing his grog,
    And he marked him out for slaughter;
For on water he scarcely had cared for Death,
    And never on rum-and-water.

Death saw two players playing at cards,
    But the game wasn't worth a dump,
For he quickly laid them flat with a spade,
    To wait for the final trump!

CRANIOLOGY.

CRANE-IOLOGY.

'Tis strange how like a very dunce,
Man—with his bumps upon his sconce,
Has lived so long, and yet no knowledge he
Has had, till lately, of Phrenology—

Q 2

A science that by simple dint of
Head-combing he should find a hint of,
When scratching o'er those little pole-hills,
The faculties throw up like mole-hills;—
A science that, in very spite
Of all his teeth, ne'er came to light,
For tho' he knew his skull had *grinders*,
Still there turn'd up no *organ* finders,
Still sages wrote, and ages fled,
And no man's head came in his head—
Not even the pate of Erra Pater,
Knew aught about its pia mater.
At last great Dr. Gall bestirs him—
I don't know but it might be Spurzheim—
Tho' native of a dull and slow land,
And makes partition of our Poll-land;
At our Acquisitiveness guesses,
And all those necessary *nesses*
Indicative of human habits,
All burrowing in the head like rabbits.
Thus Veneration, he made known,
Had got a lodging at the Crown:
And Music (see Deville's example)
A set of chambers in the Temple:
That Language taught the tongues close by,
And took in pupils thro' the eye,
Close by his neighbour Computation,
Who taught the eyebrows numeration.

The science thus—to speak in fit
Terms—having struggled from its nit,
Was seiz'd on by a swarm of Scotchmen,
Those scientifical hotch-potch men,
Who have at least a penny dip

And wallop in all doctorship,
Just as in making broth they smatter
By bobbing twenty things in water:
These men, I say, made quick appliance
And close, to phrenologic science;
For of all learned themes whatever,
That schools and colleges deliver,
There's none they love so near the bodles,
As analyzing their own noddles;
Thus in a trice each northern blockhead
Had got his fingers in his shock head,
And of his bumps was babbling yet worse
Than poor Miss Capulet's dry wet-nurse;
Till having been sufficient rangers
Of their own heads, they took to strangers',
And found in Presbyterians' polls
The things they hated in their souls;
For Presbyterians hear with passion
Of organs join'd with veneration.
No kind there was of human pumpkin
But at its bumps it had a bumpkin;
Down to the very lowest gullion,
And oiliest scull of oily scullion.
No great man died but this they *did* do,
They begged his cranium of his widow:
No murderer died by law disaster,
But they took off his sconce in plaster;
For thereon they could show depending,
" The head and front of his offending,"
How that his philanthropic bump
Was master'd by a baser lump;
For every bump (these wags insist)
Has its direct antagonist,
Each striving stoutly to prevail,

Like horses knotted tail to tail;
And many a stiff and sturdy battle
Occurs between these adverse cattle,
The secret cause, beyond all question,
Of aches ascrib'd to indigestion,—
Whereas 'tis but two knobby rivals
Tugging together like sheer devils,
Till one gets mastery good or sinister,
And comes in like a new prime-minister.

Each bias in some master node is :—
What takes M'Adam where a road is,
To hammer little pebbles less ?
His organ of Destructiveness.
What makes great Joseph so encumber
Debate ? a lumping lump of Number :
Or Malthus rail at babies so ?
The smallness of his Philopro—
What severs man and wife ? a simple
Defect of the Adhesive pimple :
Or makes weak women go astray ?
Their bumps are more in fault than they.

These facts being found and set in order
By grave M.D.s beyond the Border,
To make them for some months eternal,
Were enter'd monthly in a journal,
That many a northern sage still writes in,
And throws his little Northern Lights in,
And proves and proves about the phrenos,
A great deal more than I or he knows.
How Music suffers, *par exemple*,
By wearing tight hats round the temple
What ills great boxers have to fear

From blisters put behind the ear:
And how a porter's Veneration
Is hurt by porter's occupation:
Whether shillelaghs in reality
May deaden Individuality:
Or tongs and poker be creative
Of alterations in th' Amative:
If falls from scaffolds make us less
Inclin'd to all Constructiveness:
With more such matters, all applying
To heads—and therefore *headifying*.

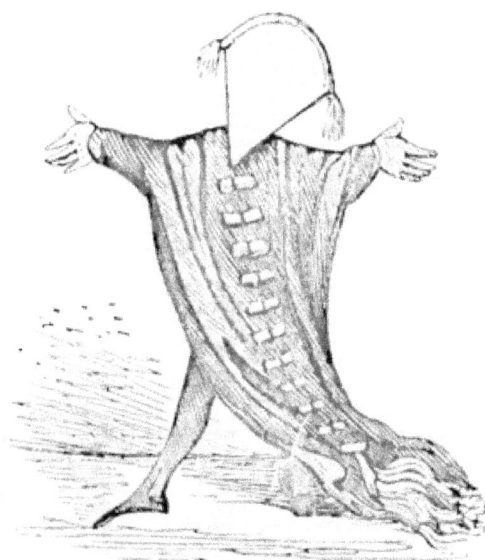

A SPECIAL PLEADER.

AN AFFAIR OF HONOUR.

"HONOUR CALLS HIM TO THE FIELD."

—— And those were the only duels," concluded the major, "that ever I fought in my life."

Now the major reminded me strongly of an old boatman at Hastings, who, after a story of a swimmer that was snapped asunder by a "sea attorney" in the West Indies, made an end in the same fashion:— "And that was the only time," said he, "I ever saw a man bit in two by a shark."

A single occurrence of the kind seemed sufficient for the experience of one life; and so I reasoned upon

the major's nine duels. He must, in the first place,
have been not only jealous and swift to quarrel; but,
in the second, have met with nine intemperate spirits
equally forward with himself. It is but in one affront
out of ten that the duellist meets with a duellist: a
computation assigning ninety mortal disagreements to
his single share; whereas I, with equal irritability
and as much courage perhaps, had never exchanged a
card in my life. The subject occupied me all the walk
homeward through the meadows :—" To get involved
in nine duels," said I : " 'tis quite improbable !"

As I thought thus, I had thrust my body halfway
under a rough bar that was doing duty for a stile at
one end of a field. It was just too high to climb
comfortably, and just low enough to be inconvenient
to duck under; but I chose the latter mode, and
began to creep through with the deliberateness
consistent with doubtful and intricate speculation.
" To get involved in nine duels—here my back hitched
a little at the bar—'tis quite impossible."

I am persuaded that there is a spirit of mischief
afoot in the world—some malignant fiend to seize
upon and direct these accidents : for just at this nick,
whilst I was boggling below the bar, there came up
another passenger by the same path : so seeing how
matters stood, he made an attempt at once to throw
his leg over the impediment : but mistaking the
altitude by a few inches, he kicked me—where I had
never been kicked before.

" By Heaven! this is too bad," said I, staggering
through head foremost from the concussion : my back
was up, in every sense, in a second.

The stranger apologised in the politest terms,—
but with such an intolerable chuckle, with such a

provoking grin lurking about his face, that I felt fury enough, like Beatrice, to "eat his heart in the market-place." In short, in two little minutes, from venting my conviction upon duelling, I found myself engaged to a meeting for the vindication of my honour.

There is a vivid description in the History of Robinson Crusoe, of the horror of the solitary Mariner at finding the mark of a foot in the sandy beach of his Desert Island. That abominable token, in a place that he fancied was sacred to himself—in a part, he made sure, never trodden by the sole of man—haunted him wherever he went. So did mine. I bore about with me the same ideal imprint—to be washed out, not by the ocean-brine, but with blood!

As I walked homeward after this adventure, and reflected on my former opinions, I felt that I had done the gallant major an injustice. It seemed likely that a man of his profession might be called out even to the ninth time—nay, that men of the peaceful cloth might, on a chance, be obliged to have recourse to mortal combat,——

As for Gentlemen *at the Bar*, I have shown how they may get into an Affair of Honour in a twinkling.

A PARTHIAN GLANCE.

A RETROSPECTIVE REVIEW.

"Sweet Memory, wafted by thy gentle gale,
Oft up the stream of time I turn my sail."

ROGERS.

I.

COME, my Crony, let's think upon far-away days,
 And lift up a little Oblivion's veil;
Let's consider the past with a lingering gaze,
 Like a peacock whose eyes are inclined to his tail.

II.

Ay, come, let us turn our attention behind,
   Like those critics whose heads are so heavy, I fear,
That they cannot keep up with the march of the mind,
   And so turn face about for reviewing the rear.

III.

Looking over Time's crupper and over his tail,
   Oh, what ages and pages there are to revise!
And as farther our back-searching glances prevail,
   Like the emmets, "how little we are in our eyes!"

IV.

What a sweet pretty innocent, half-a-yard long,
   On a dimity lap of true nursery make!
I can fancy I hear the old lullaby song
   That was meant to compose me, but kept me awake.

V.

Methinks I still suffer the infantine throes,
   When my flesh was a cushion for any long pin—
Whilst they patted my body to comfort my woes,
   Oh! how little they dreamt they were driving them in!

VI.

Infant sorrows are strong—infant pleasures as weak—
   But no grief was allow'd to indulge in its note;
Did you ever attempt a small " bubble and squeak,"
   Thro' the Dalby's Carminative down in your throat?

VII.

Did you ever go up to the roof with a bounce ?
   Did you ever come down to the floor with the same?
Oh! I can't but agree with both ends, and pronounce
   " Head or tails" with a child, an unpleasantish game!

VIII.

Then an urchin—I see myself urchin, indeed,
  With a smooth Sunday face for a mother's delight;
Why should weeks have an end ?—I am sure there
        was need
  Of a Sabbath, to follow each Saturday-night.

IX.

Was your face ever sent to the housemaid to scrub ?
  Have you ever felt huckaback soften'd with sand ?
Had you ever your nose towell'd up to a snub,
  And your eyes knuckled out with the back of the
        hand?

X.

Then a school-boy—my tailor was nothing in fault,
  For an urchin will grow to a lad by degrees,—
But how well I remember that " pepper and salt "
  That was down to the elbows, and up to the knees !

XI.

What a figure it cut when as Norval I spoke !
  With a lanky right leg duly planted before ;
Whilst I told of the chief that was kill'd by my stroke.
  And extended *my* arms as " the arms that he wore !"

XII.

Next a Lover—Oh ! say, were you ever in love ?
  With a lady too cold—and your bosom too hot !
Have you bow'd to a shoe-tie, and knelt to a glove ?
  Like a *beau* that desired to be tied in a knot ?

XIII.

With the Bride all in white, and your body in blue,
  Did you walk up the aisle—the genteelest of men ?
When I think of that beautiful vision anew,
  Oh ! I seem but the *biffin* of what I was then !

XIV.

I am wither'd and worn by a premature care,
	And my wrinkles confess the decline of my days;
Old Time's busy hand has made free with my hair,
	And I'm seeking to hide it—by writing for bays!

"MY BANKS THEY ARE FURNISHED."

A SAILOR'S APOLOGY FOR BOW-LEGS.

There's some is born with their straight legs by natur —
And some is born with bow-legs from the first—
And some that should have grow'd a good deal
    straighter,
        But they were badly nurs'd,
And set, you see, like Bacchus, with their pegs
        Astride of casks and kegs :
I've got myself a sort of bow to larboard,
        And starboard,
And this is what it was that warp'd my legs.—

'Twas all along of Poll, as I may say,
That foul'd my cable when I ought to slip ;
        But on the tenth of May,
        When I gets under weigh,
Down there in Hartfordshire, to join my ship,
        I sees the mail
        Get under sail,
The only one there was to make the trip.
        Well—I gives chase,
        But as she run
        Two knots to one,
There war'nt no use in keeping on the race !

Well—casting round about, what next to try on,
        And how to spin,
I spies an ensign with a Bloody Lion,

And bears away to leeward for the inn,
      Beats round the gable,
And fetches up before the coach-horse stable:
Well—there they stand, four kickers in a row,
        And so
I just makes free to cut a brown'un's cable.
But riding is'nt in a seaman's natur—
So I whips out a toughish end of yarn,
And gets a kind of sort of a land-waiter
        To splice me, heel to heel,
        Under the she-mare's keel,
And off I goes, and leaves the inn a-starn!

        My eyes! how she did pitch!
And would'nt keep her own to go in no line,
Tho' I kept bowsing, bowsing at her bow-line,
But always making lee-way to the ditch,
And yaw'd her head about all sorts of ways.
        The devil sink the craft!
And was'nt she trimendus slack in stays!
We could'nt, no how, keep the inn abaft!
        Well—I suppose
We had'nt run a knot—or much beyond—
(What will you have on it?)—but off she goes,
Up to her bends in a fresh-water pond!
        There I am!—all a-back!
So I looks forward for her bridle-gears,
To heave her head round on the t'other tack;
        But when I starts,
        The leather parts,
And goes away right over by the ears!

        What could a fellow do,
Whose legs, like mine, you know, were in the bilboes,

But trim myself upright for bringing-to,
And square his yard-arms, and brace up his elbows,
          In rig all snug and clever,
Just while his craft was taking in her water?
I did'nt like my burth tho', howsomdever,
Because the yarn, you see, kept getting taughter,—
Says I—I wish this job was rayther shorter!
          The chase had gain'd a mile
A-head, and still the she-mare stood a-drinking:
          Now, all the while
Her body did'nt take of course to shrinking.
Says I, she's letting out her reefs, I'm thinking—
          And so she swell'd, and swell'd,
          And yet the tackle held,
'Till both my legs began to bend like winkin.
My eyes! but she took in enough to founder!
And there's my timbers straining every bit,
          Ready to split,
And her tarnation hull a-growing rounder!

          Well, there—off Hartford Ness,
We lay both lash'd and water-logg'd together,
          And can't contrive a signal of distress;
Thinks I, we must ride out this here foul weather.
Tho' sick of riding out—and nothing less;
When, looking round, I sees a man a-starn:—
Hollo! says I, come underneath her quarter!—
And hands him out my knife to cut the yarn.
So I gets off, and lands upon the road,
And leaves the she-mare to her own concarn,
          A-standing by the water.
If I get on another, I'll be blow'd!—
And that's the way, you see, my legs got bow'd!

"NOTHING BUT HEARTS!"

"SHE IS ALL HEART."

It must have been the lot of every whist-player to observe a phenomenon at the card-table, as mysterious as any in nature—I mean the constant recurrence of a certain trump throughout the night—a run upon a particular suit, that sets all the calculations of Hoyle and Cocker at defiance. The chance of turning-up is equal to the Four Denominations. They should

alternate with each other, on the average—whereas a
Heart, perhaps, shall be the last card of every deal.
King or Queen, Ace or Deuce,—still it is of the same
clan.   You cut—and it comes again.   " Nothing but
Hearts ! "

The figure herewith might be fancied to embody
this kind of occurrence ; and, in truth, it was designed
to commemorate an evening dedicated to the same
red suit.   I had looked in by chance at the Royal
Institution : a Mr. Professor Pattison, of New York,
I believe, was lecturing, and the subject was—
" Nothing but Hearts ! "

Some hundreds of grave, curious, or scientific
personages were ranged on the benches of the Theatre ;
—every one in his solemn black.   On a table in front
of the Professor, stood the specimens : hearts of all
shapes and sizes—man's, woman's, sheep's, bullock's,
—on platters or in cloths,—were lying about as
familiar as household wares.   Drawings of hearts, in
black or blood-red, (dismal valentines !) hung around
the fearful walls.   Preparations of the organ in wax,
or bottled, passed currently from hand to hand, from
eye to eye, and returned to the gloomy table.   It was
like some solemn Egyptian Inquisition—a looking into
dead men's hearts for their morals.

The Professor began.   Each after each he displayed
the samples ; the words " auricle " and " ventricle "
falling frequently on the ear, as he explained how
those " solemn organs " pump in the human breast.
He showed, by experiments with water, the operation
of the valves with the blood, and the impossibility of
its revulsion.   As he spoke, an indescribable thrilling
or tremor crept over my left breast—thence down
my side—and all over.   I felt an awful consciousness

of the bodily presence of my heart, till then nothing
more than it is in song—a mere metaphor—so
imperceptible are all the grand vital workings of
the human frame! Now I felt the organ distinctly.
There it was!—a fleshy core—aye, like *that* on the Professor's plate—throbbing away, auricle, and ventricle,
the valve allowing the gushing blood at so many
gallons per minute, and ever prohibiting its return!

The professor proceeded to enlarge on the important
office of the great functionary, and the vital engine
seemed to dilate within me, in proportion to the sense
of its stupendous responsibility. I seemed nothing
but auricle, and ventricle, and valve. I had no
breath, but only pulsations. Those who have been
present at anatomical discussions can alone corroborate
this feeling—how the part discoursed of, by a
surpassing sympathy and sensibility, causes its
counterpart to become prominent and all-engrossing
to the sense; how a lecture on hearts makes a man
seem to himself as all heart; or one on heads causes a
Phrenologist to conceive he is " all brain."

Thus was I absorbed:—my " bosom's lord," lording
over every thing beside. By and bye, in lieu of
one solitary machine, I saw before me a congregation
of hundreds of human forcing pumps, all awfully
working together—the palpitations of hundreds of
auricles and ventricles, the flapping of hundreds
of valves! And anon they collapsed—mine—the
Professor's—those on the benches—all! all!—into
one great auricle—one great ventricle—one vast
universal heart!

The lecture ended—I took up my hat and walked
out, but the discourse haunted me. I was full of the
subject. A kind of fluttering, which was not to

be cured even by the fresh air, gave me plainly
to understand that my heart was not "in the High-
lands,"—nor in any lady's keeping—but where it
ought to be, in my own bosom, and as hard at work as
a parish pump. I plainly felt the blood—like the
carriages on a birth-night—coming in by the auricle,
and going out by the ventricle ; and shuddered to
fancy what must ensue either way, from   any
"breaking the line."   Then occurred to me the
danger of little particles absorbed in the blood,
and accumulating to a stoppage at the valve,—the
"pumps getting choked,"—a suggestion that made me
feel rather qualmish, and for relief I made a call on
Mrs. W——. The visit was ill-chosen and mistimed,
for the lady in question, by dint of good-nature, and
a romantic turn—principally estimated by her young
and female acquaintance—had acquired the reputation
of being "all heart." The phrase had often provoked
my mirth,—but, alas ! the description was now over
true. Whether nature had formed her in that mould,
or my own distempered fancy, I know not—but there
she sate, and looked the Professor's lecture over
again. She was like one of those games alluded to in
my beginning—"Nothing but Hearts !" Her nose
turned up. It was a heart—and her mouth led
a trump. Her face gave a heart—and her cap
followed suit. Her sleeves puckered and plumped
themselves into a heart-shape—and so did her body.
Her pincushion was a heart—the very back of her
chair was a heart—her bosom was a heart. She was
"all heart" indeed !

JACK HALL.

DEATH'S DOOR.

I.

'Tis very hard when men forsake
This melancholy world, and make
A bed of turf, they cannot take
　　　　A quiet doze,
But certain rogues will come and break
　　　　Their "bone repose."

II.

'Tis hard we can't give up our breath,
And to the earth our earth bequeath,
Without Death Fetches after death,
              Who thus exhume us;
And snatch us from our homes beneath,
              And hearths posthumous.

III.

The tender lover comes to rear
The mournful urn, and shed his tear—
Her glorious dust, he cries, is here!
              Alack! alack!
The while his Sacharissa dear
              Is in a sack!

IV.

'Tis hard one cannot lie amid
The mould, beneath a coffin-lid,
But thus the Faculty will bid
              Their rogues break thro' it!
If they don't want us there, why did
              They send us to it?

V.

One of these sacrilegious knaves,
Who crave as hungry vulture craves,
Behaving as the goul behaves,
              'Neath church-yard wall—
Mayhap because he fed on graves,
              Was nam'd Jack Hall!

VI.

By day it was his trade to go
Tending the black coach to and fro ;
And sometimes at the door of woe,
   With emblems suitable,
He stood with brother Mute, to show
   That life is mutable.

VII.

But long before they pass'd the ferry,
The dead that he had help'd to bury,
He sack'd—(he had a sack to carry
   The bodies off in.)
In fact, he let them have a very
   Short fit of coffin.

VIII.

Night after night, with crow and spade.
He drove this dead but thriving trade,
Meanwhile his conscience never weigh'd
   A single horsehair ;
On corses of all kinds he prey'd,
   A perfect corsair!

IX.

At last—it may be, Death took spite,
Or jesting only meant to fright—
He sought for Jack night after night
   The churchyards round ;
And soon they met, the man and sprite,
   In Pancras' ground.

X.

Jack, by the glimpses of the moon
Perceiv'd the bony knacker soon,
An awful shape to meet at noon
   Of night and lonely :
But Jack's tough courage did but swoon
   A minute only.

XI.

Anon he gave his spade a swing
Aloft, and kept it brandishing,
Ready for what mishaps might spring
   From this conjunction ;
Funking indeed was quite a thing
   Beside his function.

XII.

" Hollo!" cried Death, " d'ye wish your sands
Run out? the stoutest never stands
A chance with me,—to my commands
   The strongest truckles ;
But I'm your friend—so let's shake hands,
   I should say—knuckles."

XIII.

Jack, glad to see th' old sprite so sprightly,
And meaning nothing but uprightly,
Shook hands at once, and, bowing slightly,
   His mull did proffer :
But Death, who had no nose, politely
   Declin'd the offer.

XIV.

Then sitting down upon a bank,
Leg over leg, shank over shank,
Like friends for conversation frank,
      That had no check on :
Quoth Jack unto the Lean and Lank,
        " You're Death, I reckon."

XV.

The Jaw-bone grinn'd :—" I am that same,
You've hit exactly on my name ;
In truth it has some little fame
      Where burial sod is."
Quoth Jack, (and wink'd,) "of course ye came
      Here after bodies."

XVI.

Death grinn'd again and shook his head :—
" I've little business with the dead ;
When they are fairly sent to bed
      I've done my turn :
Whether or not the worms are fed
      Is your concern.

XVII.

" My errand here, in meeting you,
Is nothing but a ' how-d'ye do ; '
I've done what jobs I had—a few
      Along this way ;
If I can serve a crony too,
      I beg you'll say."

XVIII.

Quoth Jack, " Your Honour's very kind :
And now I call the thing to mind,
This parish very strict I find ;
       But in the next 'un
There lives a very well-inclined
       Old sort of sexton."

XIX.

Death took the hint, and gave a wink
As well as eyelet holes can blink ;
Then stretching out his arm to link
       The other's arm,—
" Suppose," says he, " we have a drink
       Of something warm."

XX.

Jack nothing loth, with friendly ease
Spoke up at once :—" Why, what ye please
Hard by there is the Cheshire Cheese,
       A famous tap."
But this suggestion seem'd to tease
       The bony chap.

XXI.

" No, no—your mortal drinks are heady,
And only make my hand unsteady ;
I do not even care for Deady,
       And loathe your rum ;
But I've some glorious brewage ready,
       My drink is—mmm !"

XXII.

And off they set, each right content—
Who knows the dreary way they went?
But Jack felt rather faint and spent.
　　　　　　And out of breath;
At last he saw, quite evident,
　　　　　　The Door of Death.

XXIII.

All other men had been unmann'd
To see a coffin on each hand,
That served a skeleton to stand
　　　　　　By way of sentry;
In fact, Death has a very grand
　　　　　　And awful entry.

XXIV.

Throughout his dismal sign prevails,
His name is writ in coffin nails;
The mortal darts make area rails;
　　　　　　A scull that mocketh,
Grins on the gloomy gate, and quails
　　　　　　Whoever knocketh.

XXV.

And lo! on either side, arise
Two monstrous pillars—bones of thighs;
A monumental slab supplies
　　　　　　The step of stone,
Where waiting for his master lies
　　　　　　A dog of bone.

XXVI.

The dog leapt up, but gave no yell,
The wire was pull'd, but woke no bell.
The ghastly knocker rose and fell,
      But caused no riot ;
The ways of Death, we all know well
      Are very quiet.

XXVII.

Old Bones stept in ; Jack stepp'd behind :
Quoth Death, " I really hope you'll find
The entertainment to your mind,
      As I shall treat ye—
A friend or two of goblin kind,
      I've asked to meet ye."

XXVIII.

And lo ! a crowd of spectres tall,
Like jack-a-lanterns on a wall,
Were standing—every ghastly ball
      An eager watcher.
" My friends," says Death—" friends, Mr. Hall,
      The body-snatcher."

XXIX.

Lord, what a tumult it produced,
When Mr. Hall was introduced !
Jack even, who had long been used
      To frightful things,
Felt just as if his back was sluic'd
      With freezing springs !

XXX.

Each goblin face began to make
Some horrid mouth—ape—gorgon—snake ;
And then a spectre-hag would shake
      An airy thigh-bone ;
And cried, (or seem'd to cry,) I'll break
      Your bone, with *my* bone!

XXXI.

Some ground their teeth—some seem'd to spit—
(Nothing, but nothing came of it,)
A hundred awful brows were knit
      In dreadful spite.
Thought Jack—I'm sure I'd better quit,
      Without good night.

XXXII.

One skip and hop and he was clear,
And running like a hunted deer,
As fleet as people run by fear
      Well spurr'd and whipp'd,
Death, ghosts, and all in that career
      Were quite outstripp'd.

XXXIII.

But those who live by death must die ;
Jack's soul at last prepar'd to fly ;
And when his latter end drew nigh,
      Oh! what a swarm
Of doctors came,—but not to try
      To keep him warm.

XXXIV.

No ravens ever scented prey
So early where a dead horse lay,
Nor vultures sniff'd so far away
        A last convulse :
A dozen " guests " day after day
        Were " at his pulse."

XXXV.

'Twas strange, altho' they got no fees,
How still they watch'd by twos and threes :
But Jack a very little ease
        Obtain'd from them ;
In fact he did not find M. D.s
        Worth one D—M.

XXXVI.

The passing bell with hollow toll
Was in his thought—the dreary hole!
Jack gave his eyes a horrid roll,
        And then a cough :—
" There's something weighing on my soul
        I wish was off ;

XXXVII.

" All night it roves about my brains,
All day it adds to all my pains,
It is concerning my remains
        When I am dead :"
Twelve wigs and twelve gold-headed canes
        Drew near his bed.

XXXVIII.

" Alas !" he sigh'd, " I'm sore afraid,
A dozen pangs my heart invade ;
But when I drove a certain trade
      In flesh and bone,
There was a little bargain made
      About my own."

XXXIX.

Twelve suits of black began to close,
Twelve pair of sleek and sable hose,
Twelve flowing cambric frills in rows,
      At once drew round ;
Twelve noses turn'd against his nose,
      Twelve snubs profound.

XL.

" Ten guineas did not quite suffice,
And so I sold my body twice ;
Twice did not do—I sold it thrice,
      Forgive my crimes !
In short I have received its price
      A dozen times !"

XLI.

Twelve brows got very grim and black,
Twelve wishes stretched him on the rack,
Twelve pair of hands for fierce attack
      Took up position,
Ready to share the dying Jack
      By long division.

XLII.

Twelve angry doctors wrangled so,
That twelve had struck an hour ago,
Before they had an eye to throw
   On the departed ;
Twelve heads turn'd round at once, and lo !
   Twelve doctors started.

XLIII.

Whether some comrade of the dead,
Or Satan took it in his head
To steal the corpse—the corpse had fled !
   'Tis only written,
That "*there was nothing in the bed,*
   But twelve were bitten !"

"WHY DON'T YOU GET UP BEHIND?"

s

THE WEE MAN.

A ROMANCE.

A HARD ROW.

———✦———

It was a merry company,
  And they were just afloat,
When lo! a man, of dwarfish span,
  Came up and hail'd the boat.

"Good morrow to ye, gentle folks,
  And will you let me in?—
A slender space will serve my case,
  For I am small and thin."

They saw he was a dwarfish man,
  And very small and thin ;
Not seven such would matter much,
  And so they took him in.

They laugh'd to see his little hat,
  With such a narrow brim ;
They laugh'd to note his dapper coat
  With skirts so scant and trim.

But barely had they gone a mile,
  When, gravely, one and all,
At once began to think the man
  Was not so very small.

His coat had got a broader skirt,
  His hat a broader brim,
His leg grew stout, and soon plump'd out
  A very proper limb.

Still on they went, and as they went,
  More rough the billows grew,—
And rose and fell, a greater swell,
  And he was swelling too !

And lo ! where room had been for seven,
  For six there scarce was space !
For five !—for four !—for three !—not more
  Than two could find a place !

There was not even room for one !
  They crowded by degrees—
Aye—closer yet, till elbows met,
  And knees were jogging knees.

"Good sir, you must not sit a-stern,
　　The wave will else come in!"
Without a word he gravely stirr'd,
　　Another seat to win.

"Good sir, the boat has lost her trim,
　　You must not sit a-lee!"
With smiling face, and courteous grace,
　　The middle seat took he.

But still, by constant quiet growth,
　　His back became so wide,
Each neighbour wight, to left and right,
　　Was thrust against the side.

Lord! how they chided with themselves,
　　That they had let him in;
To see him grow so monstrous now,
　　That came so small and thin.

On every brow a dew-drop stood,
　　They grew so scared and hot,—
"I' the name of all that's great and tall,
　　Who are ye, sir, and what?"

Loud laugh'd the Gogmagog, a laugh
　　As loud as giant's roar—
"When first I came, my proper name
　　Was Little—now I'm *Moore!*"

PYTHAGOREAN FANCIES.

FINN'S CONFERENCE WITH THE NATIVES.

Of all creeds—after the Christian—I incline most
to the Pythagorean. I like the notion of inhabiting
the body of a bird. It is the next thing to being a
cherub—at least, according to the popular image of a
boy's head and wings; a fancy that savours strangely
of the Pythagorean.

I think nobly of the soul with Malvolio, but not so

meanly, as he does by implication, of a bird-body.
What disparagement would it seem to shuffle off a
crippled, palsied, languid, bed-ridden carcase, and find
yourself floating above the world—in a flood of sunshine—under the feathers of a Royal Eagle of the
Andes?

For a beast-body I have less relish—and yet how
many men are there who seem predestined to such an
occupancy, being in this life even more than semi-
brutal! How many human faces that at least
countenance, if they do not confirm, this part of the
Brahminical Doctrine. What apes, foxes, pigs, curs,
and cats, walk our metropolis—to say nothing of him
shambling along Carnaby or Whitechapel—

A BUTCHER!

Whoe'er has gone thro' London Street,
Has seen a Butcher gazing at his meat,
    And how he keeps
    Gloating upon a sheep's
Or bullock's personals, as if his own;
    How he admires his halves
    And quarters—and his calves,
As if in truth upon his own legs grown;—
    His fat! *his* suet!
His kidneys peeping elegantly thro' it!
    His thick flank!
    And *his* thin!
      His shank!
      His shin!
Skin of his skin, and bone too of his bone!

With what an air
He stands aloof, across the thoroughfare
Gazing—and will not let a body by,
Tho' buy! buy! buy! be constantly his cry;
Meanwhile with arms a-kimbo, and a pair
Of Rhodian legs, he revels in a stare
At his Joint Stock—for one may call it so,
    Howbeit without a *Co.*
The dotage of self-love was never fonder
Than he of his brute bodies all a-row;
Narcissus in the wave did never ponder
    With love so strong,
    On his " portrait charmant,"
As our vain Butcher on his carcase yonder.

    Look at his sleek round skull!
How bright his cheek, how rubicund his nose is!
    His visage seems to be
    Ripe for beef-tea;
Of brutal juices the whole man is full—
In fact, fulfilling the metempsychosis
The Butcher is already half a Bull.

Surpassing the Butcher, in his approximation to
the brute, behold yon vagrant Hassan—a wandering
camel-driver and exhibitor, parading, for a few pence,
the creature's outlandish hump, yet burthened himself with a bunch of flesh between the shoulders.
For the sake of the implicit moral merely, or as an
illustration of comparative physiology, the show is
valuable; but as an example of the Pythagorean

dispensation, it is above appraisement. The retributive metamorphosis has commenced—the Beast has set his seal upon the Human Form—a little further, and he will be ready for a halter and a show-man.

COMPARATIVE PHYSIOLOGY.

As there are instances of men thus transmuting into the brute; so there are brutes, that, by peculiar human manners and resemblance, seem to hint at a former and a better condition. The ouran-outang, and the monkey, notoriously claim this relationship; and there are other tribes, and in particular some which use the erect posture, that are apt to provoke such Pythagorean associations. For example: —I could never read of the great William Penn's interview with the American savages, or look on the painting commemorative of that event, without dreaming that I had seen it acted over again at the meeting of a tribe of Kangaroos and a Penguin. The Kangaroos, sharp-sighted, vigilant, cunning, wild, swift, and active, as the Indians themselves;—the Penguin, very sleek, guiltless of arms, very taciturn, very sedate, except when jumping; upright in its conduct—a perfect Quaker. It confirmed me, in this last fancy, to read of the conduct of these gentle birds when assaulted, formerly, with long poles, by the seamen of Captain Cook—buffetings which the Penguins took quietly on either cheek, or side of the head, and died as meekly and passively as the primitive Martyrs of the Sect!

It is difficult to say to what excesses the desire of fresh victual, after long salt junketting, may drive a mariner; for my own part, I could not have handled a pole in that persecution without strong Pythagorean misgivings.

There is a Juvenile Poem,—"The Notorious Glutton," by Miss Taylor of Ongar, in which a duck falls sick and dies in a very human-like way. I could never eat duck for some time after the perusal of those verses;—it seemed as if in reality the soul of my grandam might inhabit such a bird. In mere tenderness to past womanhood, I could never lay the death-scene elsewhere than in a lady's chamber—with the body of the invalid propped up by comfortable pillows on a nursery chair. The sick attendant seemed one that had relished drams aforetime —had been pompously officious at human dissolutions, and would announce that "all was over!" with the same flapping of paws and duck-like inflections of tone. As for the Physician, he was an

Ex-Quack of our own kind, just called in from the pond —a sort of Man-Drake, and formerly a brother by nature, as now by name, of the author of " Winter Nights."

THE LAST VISIT.

"DON'T YOU SMELL FIRE?"

I.

Run!—run for St. Clements's engine!
  For the Pawnbroker's all in a blaze,
And the pledges are frying and singing—
  Oh! how the poor pawners will craze!

Now where can the turncock be drinking ?
   Was there ever so thirsty an elf ?—
But he still may tope on, for I'm thinking
   That the plugs are as dry as himself.

II.

The engines !—I hear them come rumbling ;
   There's the Phœnix ! the Globe! and the Sun!
What a row there will be, and a grumbling
   When the water don't start for a run !
See ! there they come racing and tearing,
   All the street with loud voices is fill'd;
Oh ! it's only the firemen a-swearing
   At a man they've run over and kill'd !

III.

How sweetly the sparks fly away now,
   And twinkle like stars in the sky ;
It's a wonder the engines don't play now,
   But I never saw water so shy !
Why there isn't enough for a snipe,
   And the fire it is fiercer, alas !
Oh ! instead of the New River pipe,
   They have gone—that they have—to the gas !

IV.

Only look at the poor little P——'s
   On the roof—is there anything sadder ?
My dears, keep fast hold, if you please,
   And they won't be an hour with the ladder !
But if any one's hot in their feet,
   And in very great haste to be saved,
Here's a nice easy bit in the street,
   That M'Adam has lately unpaved !

v.

There is some one—I see a dark shape
   At that window, the hottest of all,—
My good woman, why don't you escape ?
   Never think of your bonnet and shawl :
If your dress isn't perfect, what is it
   For once in a way to your hurt ?
When your husband is paying a visit
   There, at Number Fourteen, in his shirt !

vi.

Only see how she throws out her *chaney !*
   Her basons, and teapots, and all
The most brittle of *her* goods—or any,
   But they all break in breaking their fall :
Such things are not surely the best
   From a two-story window to throw—
She might save a good iron-bound chest,
   For there's plenty of people below !

vii.

O dear ! what a beautiful flash !
   How it shone thro' the window and door ;
We shall soon hear a scream and a crash,
   When the woman falls thro' with the floor
There ! there ! what a volley of flame,
   And then suddenly all is obscured !—
Well—I'm glad in my heart that I came ;—
   But I hope the poor man is insured !

THE VOLUNTEER.

THE ANGEL OF DEATH.

"The clashing of my armour in my ears
Sounds like a passing bell; my buckler puts me
In mind of a bier; this, my broadsword, a pickaxe
To dig my grave."   THE LOVER'S PROGRESS

I.

'Twas in that memorable year
France threaten'd to put off in
Flat-bottom'd boats, intending each
To be a British coffin,
To make sad widows of our wives,
And every babe an orphan:—

II.

When coats were made of scarlet cloaks,
And heads were dredg'd with flour,
I listed in the Lawyers' Corps,
Against the battle hour;
A perfect Volunteer—for why?
I brought my "will and pow'r."

III.

One dreary day—a day of dread,
Like Cato's, over-cast—
About the hour of six, (the morn
And I were breaking fast,)
There came a loud and sudden sound,
That struck me all aghast!

IV.

A dismal sort of morning roll,
That was not to be eaten:
Although it was no skin of mine,
But parchment that was beaten,
I felt tattoo'd through all my flesh,
Like any Otaheitan.

V.

My jaws with utter dread enclosed
The morsel I was munching,
And terror lock'd them up so tight,
My very teeth went crunching
All through my bread and tongue at once,
Like sandwich made at lunching.

VI.

My hand that held the tea-pot fast,
Stiffen'd, but yet unsteady,
Kept pouring, pouring, pouring o'er
The cup in one long eddy,
Till both my hose were mark'd with *tea*,
As they were mark'd already.

VII.

I felt my visage turn from red
To white—from cold to hot ;
But it was nothing wonderful
My colour changed, I wot,
For, like some variable silks,
I felt that I was shot.

VIII.

And looking forth with anxious eye,
From my snug upper story,
I saw our melancholy corps,
Going to beds all gory ;
The pioneers seem'd very loth
To axe their way to glory.

IX.

The captain march'd as mourners march,
The ensign too seem'd lagging,
And many more, although they were
No ensigns, took to flagging—
Like corpses in the Serpentine,
Methought they wanted dragging.

X.

But while I watch'd, the thought of death
Came like a chilly gust,
And lo! I shut the window down,
With very little lust
To join so many marching men,
That soon might be March dust.

XI.

Quoth I, "since Fate ordains it so.
Our foe the coast must land on;"—
I felt so warm beside the fire
I cared not to abandon;
Our hearths and homes are always things
That patriots make a stand on.

XII.

"The fools that fight abroad for home,"
Thought I, "may get a wrong one;
Let those that have no homes at all,
Go battle for a long one."
The mirror here confirm'd me this
Reflection, by a strong one.

XIII.

For there, where I was wont to shave,
And deck me like Adonis,
There stood the leader of our foes,
With vultures for his cronies—
No Corsican, but Death himself,
The Bony of all Bonies.

T

XIV.

A horrid sight it was, and sad
To see the grisly chap
Put on my crimson livery,
And then begin to clap
My helmet on—ah me! it felt
Like any felon's cap.

XV.

My plume seem'd borrow'd from a hearse,
An undertaker's crest;
My epaulettes like coffin-plates;
My belt so heavy press'd,
Four pipeclay cross-roads seem'd to lie
At once upon my breast.

XVI.

My brazen breast-plate only lack'd
A little heap of salt,
To make me like a corpse full dress'd,
Preparing for the vault—
To set up what the Poet calls
My everlasting halt.

XVII.

This funeral show inclined me quite
To peace :—and here I am !
Whilst better lions go to war,
Enjoying with the lamb
A lengthen'd life, that might have been
A martial epigram.

A MARRIAGE PROCESSION.

BRIDE AND BRIDESMAID.

It has never been my lot to marry—whatever I may have written of one Honoria to the contrary. My affair with that lady never reached beyond a very embarrassing declaration, in return for which she breathed into my dull deaf ear an inaudible answer. It was beyond my slender assurance, in those days, to ask for a repetition, whether of acceptance or denial.

T 2

One chance for explanation still remained. I wrote to her mother, to bespeak her sanction to our union, and received, by return of post, a scrawl, that, for aught I knew, might be in Sanscrit. I question whether, even at this time, my intolerable bashfulness would suffer me to press such a matter any farther.

My thoughts of matrimony are now confined to occasional day-dreams, originating in some stray glimpse in the Prayer Book, or the receipt of bride-cake. It was on some such occurrence that I fell once, Bunyan-like, into an allegory of a wedding.

My fancies took the order of a procession. With flaunting banners it wound its Alexandrine way—in the manner of some of Martin's painted pageants—to a taper spire in the distance. And first, like a band of livery, came the honourable company of Match-makers, all mature spinsters and matrons—and as like aunts and mothers as may be. The Glovers trod closely on their heels. Anon came, in blue and gold, the parish beadle, Scarabæus Parochialis, with the ringers of the hand-bells. Then came the Banns—it was during the reign of Lord Eldon's Act—three sturdy pioneers, with their three axes, and likely to hew down sterner impediments than lie commonly in the path of marriage. On coming nearer, the countenance of the first was right foolish and perplext; of the second, simpering; and the last, methought, looked sedate, as if dashed with a little fear. After the banns—like the judges following the halberts—came the joiners: no rough mechanics, but a portly, full-blown vicar, with his clerk—both rubicund—a peony paged by a pink. It made me smile to observe the droll clerical turn of the clerk's beaver scrubbed into that fashion

by his coat, at the nape. The marriage-knot—borne
by a ticket-porter—came after the divine, and raised
associations enough to sadden one, but for a pretty
Cupid that came on laughing and trundling a hoop-
ring.

JOINERS.

The next group was a numerous one, Firemen of
the Hand-in-Hand, with the Union flag—the chief
actors were near. With a mixture of anxiety and
curiosity, I looked out for the impending couple,
when, how shall I tell it? I beheld, not a brace of
young lovers—a Romeo and Juliet, not a "he-moon
here, and a she-sun there"—not bride and bridegroom
—but the happy *pear*, a solitary Bergamy, carried
on a velvet cushion by a little foot-page. I could

have foresworn my fancy for ever for so wretched
a conceit, till I remembered that it was intended,
perhaps, to typify, under that figure, the mysterious
resolution of two into one, a pair nominally, but in
substance single, which belongs to marriage. To
make amends, the high contracting parties approached
in proper person—a duplication sanctioned by the
practice of the oldest masters in their historical
pictures. It took a brace of Cupids, with a halter, to
overcome the "sweet reluctant delay" of the Bride,
and make her keep pace with the procession. She was
absorbed like a nun, in her veil; tears, too, she dropped,
large as sixpences, in her path; but her attendant
bridesmaid put on such a coquettish look, and tripped
along so airily, that it cured all suspicion of heart-
ache in such maiden showers. The Bridegroom, drest
for the Honeymoon, was ushered by Hymen—a little
link-boy; and the imp used the same importunity for
his dues. The next was a motley crew. For nuptial
ode or *Carmen*, there walked two carters, or draymen,
with their whips; a leash of footmen in livery indi-
cated Domestic Habits; and Domestic Comfort was
personated by an ambulating advertiser of "Hot
Dinners every Day."

I forget whether the Bride's Character preceded
or followed her—but it was a lottery placard, and
blazoned her as One of Ten Thousand. The parents
of both families had a quiet smile on their faces,
hinting that their enjoyment was of a retrospective
cast; and as for the six sisters of the bride, they
would have wept with her, but that six young gallants
came after them. The friends of the family were
Quakers, and seemed to partake of the happiness of

the occasion in a very quiet and quaker-like way. I
ought to mention that a band of harmonious sweet
music preceded the Happy Pair. There was none
came after—the veteran, Townsend, with his constables,
to keep order, making up the rear of the Procession.

THE MAN IN THE HONEYMOON.

THE WIDOW.

"ENCOMPASS'D IN AN ANGEL'S FRAME."

ONE widow at a grave will sob
A little while, and weep, and sigh!
If two should meet on such a job,
They'll have a gossip by and by.
If three should come together—why,
Three widows are good company!
If four should meet by any chance,
Four is a number very nice,

To have a rubber in a trice—
But five will up and have a dance!

Poor Mrs. C———(why should I not
Declare her name?—her name was Cross)
Was one of those the " common lot "
Had left to weep " no common loss ; "—
For she had lately buried then
A man, the "very best of men,"
A lingering truth, discover'd first
Whenever men "are at the worst."
To take the measure of her woe,
It was some dozen inches deep—
I mean in crape, and hung so low,
It hid the drops she did *not* weep:
In fact, what human life appears,
It was a perfect " veil of tears."
Though ever since she lost "her prop
And stay,"—alas! he wouldn't stay—
She never had a tear to mop,
Except one little angry drop,
From Passion's eye, as Moore would say;
Because, when Mister Cross took flight,
It look'd so very like a spite—
He died upon a washing-day!

Still Widow Cross went twice a week,
As if " to wet a widow's cheek,"
And soothe his grave with sorrow's gravy, —
'Twas nothing but a make-believe,
She might as well have hoped to grieve
Enough of brine to float a navy ;
And yet she often seem'd to raise
A cambric kerchief to her eye—

A *duster* ought to be the phrase,
Its work was all so very dry.
The springs were lock'd that ought to flow—
In England or in widow-woman—
As those that watch the weather know,
Such " backward Springs " are not uncommon.

But why did Widow Cross take pains,
To call upon the " dear remains,"—
Remains that could not tell a jot,
Whether she ever wept or not,
Or how his relict took her losses ?
Oh ! my black ink turns red for shame—
But still the naughty world must learn,
There was a little German came
To shed a tear in " Anna's Urn,"
At the next grave to Mr. Cross's !
For there an angel's virtues slept,
" Too soon did Heaven assert its claim ! "
But still her painted face he kept,
" Encompass'd in an angel's frame."

He look'd quite sad and quite deprived,
His head was nothing but a hat-band ;
He look'd so lone, and so *unwived*,
That soon the Widow Cross contrived
To fall in love with even *that* band ;
And all at once the brackish juices
Came gushing out thro' sorrow's sluices—
Tear after tear too fast to wipe,
Tho' sopp'd, and sopp'd, and sopp'd again—
No leak in sorrow's private pipe,
But like a bursting on the main !
Whoe'er has watch'd the window-pane—

I mean to say in showery weather—
Has seen two little drops of rain,
Like lovers very fond and fain,
At one another creeping, creeping,
Till both, at last, embrace together :
So far'd it with that couple's weeping!
The principle was quite as active—
  Tear unto tear,
  Kept drawing near,
Their very blacks became attractive.
To cut a shortish story shorter,
Conceive them sitting tête à tête—
Two cups,—hot muffins on a plate,—
With " Anna's Urn " to hold hot water!
The brazen vessel for a while,
Had lectured in an easy song,
Like Abernethy—on the bile—
The scalded herb was getting strong ;
All seem'd as smooth as smooth could be,
To have a cosey cup of tea ;
Alas! how often human sippers
With unexpected bitters meet,
And buds, the sweetest of the sweet,
Like sugar, only meet the nippers!

The Widow Cross, I should have told,
Had seen three husbands to the mould ;
She never sought an Indian pyre,
Like Hindoo wives that lose their loves,
But with a proper sense of fire,
Put up, instead, with " three removes : "
Thus, when with any tender words
Or tears she spoke about her loss,
The dear departed, Mr. Cross,

Came in for nothing but his thirds ;
For, as all widows love too well,
She liked upon the list to dwell,
And oft ripp'd up the old disasters—
She might, indeed, have been supposed
A great *ship* owner, for she prosed
Eternally of her Three Masters!

Thus, foolish woman! while she nursed
Her mild souchong, she talk'd and reckon'd
What had been left her by her first,
And by her last, and by her second.
Alas! not all her annual rents
Could then entice the little German,—
Not Mr. Cross's Three Per Cents,
Or Consols, ever make him *her* man ;
He liked her cash, he liked her houses,
But not that dismal bit of land
She always settled on her spouses.
So taking up his hat and band,
Said he " You'll think my conduct odd—
But here my hopes no more may linger ;
I thought you had a wedding-finger,
But oh !—it is a curtain-rod ! "

A MAD DOG

Is none of my bug-bears. Of the bite of dogs, large ones especially, I have a reasonable dread; but as to any participation in the canine frenzy, I am somewhat sceptical. The notion savours of the same fanciful superstition that invested the subjects of Dr. Jenner with a pair of horns. Such was affirmed to be the effect of the vaccine matter—and I shall believe what I have heard of the canine virus, when I see a rabid gentleman, or gentlewoman, with flap-ears, dew-claws, and a brush-tail!

I lend no credit to the imputed effects of a mad dog's saliva. We hear of none such amongst the West Indian Negroes—and yet their condition is always *slavery*.

I put no faith in the vulgar stories of human beings betaking themselves, through a dog-bite, to dog-habits: and consider the smotherings and drownings, that have originated in that fancy, as cruel as the murders for witchcraft. Are we, for a few yelpings, to stifle all the disciples of Loyola—Jesuit's Bark—or plunge unto death all the convalescents who may take to bark and wine?

As for the Hydrophobia, or loathing of water, I have it mildly myself. My head turns invariably at thin washy potations. With a dog, indeed, the case is different—he is a water-drinker; and when he takes to grape-juice, or the stronger cordials, may be

dangerous. But I have never seen one with a bottle
—except at his tail.

There are other dogs who are born to haunt the
liquid element, to dive and swim—and for such
to shun the lake or the pond would look suspicious.
A Newfoundlander, standing up from a shower at a
door-way, or a Spaniel with a Parapluie, might be innocently destroyed. But when does such a cur occur.

HYDROPHOBIA.

There are persons, however, who lecture on
Hydrophobia very dogmatically. It is one of their
maggots, that if a puppy be not wormed, he is
apt to go rabid. As if forsooth it made so much
difference, his merely speaking or not with, what
Lord Duberly calls, his " vermicular tongue ; " Verily,
as Izaak Walton would say, these gudgeons take the
worm very kindly !

Next to a neglect of calling in Dr. Gardner, want
of water is prone to drive a dog mad. A reasonable
saying—but the rest is not so plausible, viz. that
if you keep a dog till he is very dry, he will refuse to
drink. It is a gross libel on the human-like instinct
of the animal, to suppose him to act so clean contrary
to human-kind. A crew of sailors, thirsting at sea,
will suck their pumps or the canvass—any thing
that will afford a drop of moisture; whereas a parching
dog, instead of cooling his tongue at the next gutter,
or licking his own kennel for imaginary relief, runs
senselessly up and down to over-heat himself, and
resents the offer of a bucket like a mortal affront.
Away he scuds, straight forward like a marmot—except
when he dodges a pump. A glimmering instinct guides
him to his old haunts. He bites his Ex-master—grips
his trainer—takes a snap with a friend or two where
he used to visit—and then biting right and left
at the public, at last dies—a pitchfork in his eye,
fifty slugs in his ribs, and a spade through the small
of his back.

The career of the animal is but a type of his
victim's—suppose some Bank Clerk. He was not
bitten, but only splashed on the hand by the mad
foam or dog-spray: a recent flea-bite gives entrance
to the virus, and in less than three years it gets
possession. Then the tragedy begins. The unhappy
gentleman first evinces uneasiness at being called
on for his New River rates. He answers the
Collector snappishly, and when summoned to pay for
his supply of water, tells the Commissioners doggedly,
that they may cut it off. From that time he gets
worse. He refuses slops—turns up a pug nose at
pump-water—and at last, on a washing-day, after

flying at the laundress, rushes out, ripe for hunting,
to the street. A twilight remembrance leads him
to the house of his intended. He fastens on her
hand—next worries his mother—takes a bit apiece
out of his brothers and sisters—runs a-muck, "giving
tongue," all through the suburbs—and finally, is
smothered by a pair of bed-beaters in Moorfields.

According to popular theory the mischief ends
not here. The dog's master—the trainer, the friends,
human and canine—the Bank Clerks—the laundresses
—sweetheart—mother and sisters—the two bed-
beaters—all inherit the rabies, and run about to bite
others. It is a wonder, the madness increasing by
this ratio, that examples are not running in packs
at every turn :—my experience, nothwithstanding,
records but one instance.

It was my Aunt's brute. His temper, latterly,
had altered for the worse, and in a sullen, or insane
fit, he made a snap at the cook's radish-like fingers.
The act demanded an inquest De Lunatico Inquirendo
—he was lugged neck and crop to a full bucket ; but
you may bring a horse to the water, says the Proverb,
yet not make him drink, and the cur asserted the
same independence. To make sure, Betty cast
the whole gallon over him, a favour that he received
with a mood that would have been natural in any
mortal. His growl was conclusive. The cook alarmed,
first the family, and then the neighbourhood, which
poured all its males capable of bearing arms into
the passage. There were sticks, staves, swords, and a
gun, a prong or two, moreover, glistened here and
there. The kitchen-door was occupied by the first
rank of the column, their weapons all bristling in
advance ; and right opposite—at the further side

of the kitchen, and holding all the army at bay—stood
Hydrophobia—" in its most dreadful form!"

Conceive, Mulready! under this horrible figure
of speech, a round, goggle-eyed pug-face, supported by
two stumpy bandy-legs—the forelimbs of a long,
pampered, sausage-like body, that rested on a similar
pair of crotchets at the other end! Not without
short wheezy pantings, he began to waddle towards
the guarded entry—but before he had accomplished
a quarter of the distance, there resounded the report
of a musket. The poor Turnspit gave a yell—the
little brown bloated body tumbled over, pierced by a
dozen slugs, but not mortally; for before the piece
could be reloaded, he contrived to lap up a little pool
—from Betty's bucket—that had settled beside the
hearth.

"SPEAK UP, SIR!"

JOHN TROT.

A BALLAD.

DRILL AND BROADCAST.

I.

JOHN TROT he was as tall a lad
  As York did ever rear—
As his dear Granny used to say,
  He'd make a grenadier.

II.

A serjeant soon came down to York,
  With ribbons and a frill;
My lads, said he, let broadcast be,
  And come away to drill.

III.

But when he wanted John to 'list,
  In war he saw no fun,
Where what is call'd a raw recruit,
  Gets often over-done.

IV.

Let others carry guns, said he,
  And go to war's alarms,
But I have got a shoulder-knot
  Impos'd upon my arms.

V.

For John he had a footman's place
  To wait on Lady Wye—
She was a dumpy woman, tho'
  Her family was high.

VI.

Now when two years had past away,
  Her Lord took very ill,
And left her to her widowhood,
  Of course more dumpy still.

VII.

Said John, I am a proper man,
  And very tall to see;
Who knows, but now her Lord is low,
  She may look up to me?

VIII.

A cunning woman told me once,
　Such fortune would turn up;
She was a kind of sorceress,
　But studied in a cup!

IX.

So he walk'd up to Lady Wye,
　And took her quite amazed,—
She thought, tho' John was tall enough,
　He wanted to be raised.

X.

But John—for why? she was a dame
　Of such a dwarfish sort—
Had only come to bid her make
　Her mourning very short.

XI.

Said he, your Lord is dead and cold,
　You only cry in vain;
Not all the Cries of London now,
　Could call him back again!

XII.

You'll soon have many a noble beau,
　To dry your noble tears—
But just consider this, that I
　Have follow'd you for years.

XIII.

And tho' you are above me far,
　What matters high degree,
When you are only four foot nine,
　And I am six foot three?

XIV.

For tho' you are of lofty race,
    And I'm a low-born elf;
Yet none among your friends could say,
    You matched beneath yourself.

XV.

Said she, such insolence as this
    Can be no common case;
Tho' you are in my service, sir,
    Your love is out of place.

XVI.

O Lady Wye! O Lady Wye!
    Consider what you do;
How can you be so short with me,
    I am not so with you!

XVII.

Then ringing for her serving men,
    They show'd him to the door:
Said they, you turn out better now,
    Why didn't you before?

XVIII.

They stripp'd his coat, and gave him kicks
    For all his wages due;
And off, instead of green and gold,
    He went in black and blue.

XIX.

No family would take him in,
    Because of this discharge;
So he made up his mind to serve
    The country all at large.

XX.

Huzza! the Serjeant cried, and put
   The money in his hand,
And with a shilling cut him off
   From his paternal land.

XXI.

For when his regiment went to fight
   At Saragossa town,
A Frenchman thought he look'd too tall,
   And so he cut him down!

HIGH-BORN AND LOW-BORN.

AN ABSENTEE.

— ✦ —

IF ever a man wanted a flapper—no Butcher's
mimosa, or catch-fly, but one of those officers in use
at the court of Laputa—my friend W——should have
such a remembrancer at his elbow. I question whether
even the appliance of a bladder full of peas, or pebbles,
would arouse him from some of his abstractions—fits
of mental insensibility, parallel with those bodily
trances in which persons have sometimes been coffined.
Not that he is entangled in abstruse problems, like the
nobility of the Flying Island! He does not dive, like
Sir Isaac Newton, into a reverie, and turn up again
with a Theory of Gravitation. His thoughts are not
deeply engaged elsewhere—they are nowhere. His
head revolves itself, top-like, into a profound slumber:
—a blank doze without a dream. He is not carried
away by incoherent rambling fancies, out of himself,—
he is not drunk, merely, with the Waters of Oblivion,
but drowned in them, body and soul!

There is a story, somewhere, of one of these absent
persons, who stooped down, when tickled about the
calf by a blue-bottle, and scratched his neighbour's leg:
an act of tolerable forgetfulness, but denoting a state
far short of W——'s absorptions. He would never
have felt the fly.

To make W——'s condition more whimsical, he

lives in a small bachelor's house, with no other attendant than an old housekeeper—one Mistress Bundy,
of faculty as infirm and intermitting as his own.   It
will be readily believed that her absent fits do not
originate, any more than her master's, in abstruse
mathematical speculations—a proof with me that such
moods result, not from abstractions of mind, but
stagnation.   How so ill-sorted a couple contrive to
get through the common-place affairs of life, I am
not prepared to say: but it is comical indeed to see
him ring up Mistress Bundy to receive orders, which
he generally forgets to deliver—or if delivered, this
old Bewildered Maid lets slip out of her remembrance
with the same facility.   Numberless occurrences of
this kind—in many instances more extravagant—
are recorded by his friends; but an evening that I
spent with him recently, will furnish an abundance of
examples.

In spite of going by his own invitation, I found
W—— within. He was too apt, on such occasions,
to be denied to his visitors; but what in others would
be an unpardonable affront, was overlooked in a man
who was not always at home to himself. The door
was opened by the housekeeper, whose absence, as
usual, would not allow her to decide upon that of her
master. Her shrill quavering voice went echoing up
stairs with its old query,—"Mr. W——! are you
within?" then a pause, literally for him to collect
himself. Anon came his answer, and I was ushered
up stairs, Mrs. Bundy contriving, as usual, to forget
my name at the first landing-place. I had therefore to
introduce myself formally to W——, whose old friends
came to him always as if with new faces. As for
what followed, it was one of the old fitful colloquies

—a game at conversation, sometimes with a partner,
sometimes with a dummy; the old woman's memory
in the meantime growing torpid on a kitchen-chair.
Hour after hour passed away: no tea-spoon jingled,
or tea-cup rattled; no murmuring kettle or hissing
urn found its way upward from one Haunt of Forgetfulness to the other. In short, as might have been
expected with an Absentee, the Tea was absent.

It happens that the meal in question is not one of
my essentials; I therefore never hinted at the In Tea
Speravi of my visit; but at the turn of eleven o'clock,
my host rang for the apparatus. The Chinese ware
was brought up, but the herb was deficient. Mrs.
Bundy went forth, by command, for a supply; but it
was past grocer-time, and we arranged to make
amends by an early supper, which came, however, as
proportionably late as the tea. By dint of those
freedoms which you must use with an entertainer who is
absent at his own table, I contrived to sup sparely;
and W——'s memory, blossoming like certain flowers
to the night, reminded him that I was accustomed to
go to bed on a tumbler of Geneva and water. He
kept but one bottle of each of the three kinds, Rum,
Brandy, and Hollands, in the house; and when
exhausted they were replenished at the tavern a few
doors off. Luckily, for it was far beyond the midnight
hour when, according to our vapid magistracy, all
spirits are evil, the three vessels were full, and merely
wanted bringing up stairs. The kettle was singing on
the hob: the tumblers, with spoons in them, stood
miraculously ready on the board; and Mrs. Bundy
was really on her way from below with the one thing
needful. Never were fair hopes so unfairly blighted!
I could hear her step labouring on the stairs to the

very last step, when her memory serving her just as treacherously as her forgetfulness, or rather both betraying her together, there befel the accident which I have endeavoured to record by the following sketch.

I never ate or drank with the Barmecide again!

"LAWK! I'VE FORGOT THE BRANDY!"

ODE TO THE CAMELEOPARD.

UNCONSCIOUS IMITATION.

Welcome to Freedom's birth-place—and a den!
    Great Anti-climax, hail!
So very lofty in thy front—but then,
    So dwindling at the tail!—
In truth, thou hast the most unequal legs!
Has one pair gallopp'd, whilst the other trotted,

Along with other brethren, leopard-spotted,
O'er Afric sand, where ostriches lay eggs?
Sure thou wert caught in some hard uphill chase,
Those hinder heels still keeping thee in check!
    And yet thou seem'st prepared in any case,
    Tho' they had lost the race,
      To win it by a neck!

That lengthy neck—how like a crane's it looks!
Art thou the overseer of all the brutes?
Or dost thou browze on tip-top leaves or fruits—
Or go a bird-nesting amongst the rooks?
How kindly nature caters for all wants;
Thus giving unto thee a neck that stretches,
    And high food fetches—
To some a long nose, like the elephant's!

Oh! had'st thou any organ to thy bellows,
To turn thy breath to speech in human style,
    What secrets thou might'st tell us,
Where now our scientific guesses fail;
    For instance of the Nile,
Whether those Seven Mouths have any tail—
    Mayhap thy luck too,
From that high head, as from a lofty hill,
Has let thee see the marvellous Timbuctoo—
Or drink of Niger at its infant rill;
What were the travels of our Major Denham,
    Or Clapperton, to thine
    In that same line,
If thou could'st only squat thee down and pen 'em.'

Strange sights, indeed, thou must have overlook'd,
With eyes held ever in such vantage-stations!

Hast seen, perchance, unhappy white folks cook'd,
And then made free of negro corporations?
Poor wretches saved from cast away three-deckers—
By sooty wreckers—
From hungry waves to have a loss still drearier,
To far exceed the utmost aim of Park—
And find themselves, alas! beyond the mark,
In the *insides* of Africa's Interior!

AFRICAN WRECKERS.

Live on, Giraffe! genteelest of raff kind!
Admir'd by noble, and by royal tongues!
May no pernicious wind,
Or English fog, blight thy exotic lungs!

Live on in happy peace, altho' a rarity,
Nor envy thy poor cousin's more outrageous
        Parisian popularity ;
Whose very leopard-rash is grown contagious,
And worn on gloves and ribbons all about,
        Alas ! they'll wear him out !
So thou shalt take thy sweet diurnal feeds—
When he is stuff'd with undigested straw,
Sad food that never visited his jaw !
And staring round him with a brace of beads !

WHITE BAIT.

A MAY-DAY

A MAY-DUKE.

I know not what idle schemer or mad wag put such a folly in the head of my Lady Rasherly, but she resolved to celebrate a May-day after the old fashion, and convert Porkington Park—her Hampshire Leasowes —into a new Arcadia. Such revivals have always come to a bad end: the Golden Age is not to

be regilt; Pastoral is gone out, and Pan extinct—
Pans will not last for ever.

But Lady Rasherly's fête was fixed. A large order
was sent to Ingram, of rustic celebrity, for nubbly
sofas and crooked chairs; a letter was dispatched to
the Manager of the P——h Theatre, begging a loan
from the dramatic wardrobe; and old Jenkins, the
steward, was sent through the village to assémble as
many, male and female, of the barn-door kind, as
he could muster. Happy for the Lady, had her
Hampshire peasantry been more pig-headed and
hoggishly untractable, like the staple animal of the
county: but the time came and the tenants. Happy
for her, had the goodnatured manager excused himself,
with a plea that the cottage-hats, and blue bodices,
and russet skirts, were bespoke, for that very night, by
Rosina and her villagers. But the day came and the
dresses. I am told that old Jenkins and his helpmate
had a world of trouble in the distribution of the
borrowed plumes: this maiden turning up a pug-nose,
still pugger, at a faded bodice; that damsel thrusting
out a pair of original pouting lips, still more spout-
like, at a rusty ribbon; carroty Celias wanted more
roses in their hair, and dumpy Delias more flounces
in their petticoats. There is a natural tact, however,
in womankind as to matters of dress, that made them
look tolerably when all was done: but pray except
from this praise the gardener's daughter, Dolly
Blossom,—a born sloven, with her horticultural hose,
which she had *pruned* so often at top to *graft* at
bottom, that, from long stockings, they had dwindled
into short socks; and it seemed as if, by a similar
process, she had coaxed her natural calves into her
ankles. The men were less fortunate in their toilette:

they looked slack in their tights, and tight in their slacks; to say nothing of Johnny Giles, who was so tight all over, that he looked as if he had stolen his clothes, and the clothes, turning King's evidence, were going to "*split* upon him."

In the mean time, the retainers at the Park had not been idle. The old mast was taken down from the old barn, and stripped of its weathercock, did duty as a May-pole. The trees and shrubs were hung with artificial garlands; and a large marquee made an agreeable contrast, in canvass, with the long lawn. An extempore wooden arbour had likewise been erected for the May Queen; and here stood my Lady Rasherly with her daughters: my Lady, with a full moon face, and a half moon tiara, was Diana; the young ladies represented her Nymphs, and they had all bows and arrows, Spanish hats and feathers, Lincoln green spensers and slashed sleeves,—the uniform of the Porkington Archery. There were, moreover, six younger young ladies—a loan from the parish school—who were to be the immediate attendants on her Sylvan Majesty, and, as they expressed it in their own simple Doric, "to *shy* flowers at her *fut!*"

And now the nymphs and swains began to assemble: Damon and Phillis, Strephon and Amaryllis—a nomenclature not a little puzzling to the performers, for Delia answered to Damon, and Chloe instead of Colin,—

"And, though I called another, Abra came."

But I must treat you with a few personalities. Damon was one Darius Dobbs. He was entrusted with a fine tinsel crook and half-a-dozen sheep, which

x

he was puzzled to keep, by hook, or by crook, to the
lawn ; for Corydon, his fellow shepherd, had quietly
hung up his pastoral emblem, and walked off to the
sign of the Rose and Crown. Poor Damon! there he
sat, looking the very original of Phillips's line,

> "Ah, silly I, more silly than my sheep,"

and, to add to his perplexity, he could not help seeing
and hearing Mary Jenks, his own sweetheart, who,
having no lambs to keep, was romping where she
would, and treating whom she would with a kindness
by no means sneaking. Poor Darius Dobbs!

Gregory Giles was Colin ; and he was sadly ham-
pered with "two hands out of employ ;" for, after
feeling up his back, and down his bosom, and about
his hips, he had discovered that, to save time and
trouble, his stage-clothes had been made without
pockets. But

> "Satan finds some mischief still
> For idle hands to do ; "

and, accordingly, he soon set Colin's fingers to work
so busily, that they twiddled off all the buttons from
his borrowed jacket.

Strephon was nothing particular, only a sky-blue
body on a pair of chocolate-coloured legs. But Lubin
was a jewel ! He had formerly been a private in the
Baconfield Yeomanry, and therefore thought proper
to surmount his pastoral uniform with a cavalry cap!
Such an incongruity was not to be overlooked. Old
Jenkins remonstrated, but Lubin was obstinate; the
steward persisted, and the other replied with a " posi-
tive negative ;" and, in the end, Lubin went off in a
huff to the Rose and Crown.

The force of *two* bad examples was too much for the
virtue of Darius Dobbs: he threw away his crook, left
his sheep to anybody, and ran off to the alehouse, and,
what was worse, Colin was sent after him, and never
came back!

The chief of the faithful shepherds, who now remained at the park, was Hobbinol—one Josias Strong,
a notorious glutton, who had won sundry wagers by
devouring a leg of mutton and trimmings at a sitting.
He was a big lubberly fellow, that had been born
great, and had achieved greatness, but had not greatness thrust upon him. It was as much as he could
do to keep his trowsers,—for he was at once clown
and pantaloon,—down to the knee, and more than he
could do to keep them up to the waist ; and, to crown
all, having rashly squatted down on the lawn, the
juicy herbage had left a stain behind, on his caliman-
coes, that still occupies the "greenest spot" in the
memoirs of Baconfield.

There were some half-dozen of other rustics to the
same pattern, but the fancy of my Lady Rasherly did
not confine itself to the humanities. Old Joe Bradley,
the blacksmith, was Pan; and truly he made a respect-
able satyr enough, for he came half drunk, and was
rough, gruff, tawny and brawny, and bow-legged, and
hadn't been shaved for a month. His cue was to
walk about in buckskins, leading his own billy-goat,
and he was followed up and down by his sister, Patty,
whom the wags called *Patty Pan.*

The other Deity was also a wet one—a triton
amongst mythologists, but Timothy Gubbins with his
familiars,—the acknowledged dolt of the village, and
remarkable for his weekly slumbers in the parish
church. It had been ascertained that he could

neither pipe, nor sing, nor dance, nor even keep
sheep, so he was stuck with an urn under his arm,
and a rush crown, as the God of the fish-pond,—a
task, simple as it was, that proved beyond his genius,
for, after stupidly dozing awhile over his vase, he fell
into a sound snoring sleep, out of which he cold-
pigged himself by tumbling, urn and all, into his own
fountain.

Misfortunes always come pick-a-back. The Rose
and Crown happened to be a receiving-house for the
drowned, under the patronage of the Humane Society,
wherefore the *Water God* insisted on going there *to
be dried*, and Cuddy, who pulled him out, insisted on
going with him! These two had certainly some
slight excuse for walking off to the alehouse, whereas
Sylvio thought proper to follow them without any
excuse at all!

This mischance was but the prelude of new disasters. It was necessary, before beginning the sports
of the day, to elect a MAY QUEEN, and, by the influence of Lady Rasherly, the choice of the lieges fell
upon Jenny Acres, a really pretty maiden, and worthy
of the honour; but in the meantime Dolly Wiggins,
a brazen strapping dairy-maid, had quietly elected
herself,—snatched a flower-basket from one of the six
Floras, strewed her own path, and getting first to the
royal arbour, squatted there firm and fast, and persisted in reigning as QUEEN in her own right. Hence
arose civil and uncivil war,—and Alexis and Diggon,
being interrupted in a boxing match in the Park,
adjourned to the Rose and Crown to have it out; and
as two can't make a ring, a round dozen of the shepherds went along with them for that purpose.

There now remained but five swains in Arcadia, and

they had five nymphs apiece, besides Mary Jenks, who divided her favour equally amongst them all. There should have been next in order a singing match on the lawn, for a prize, after the fashion of Pope's Pastorals; but Corydon, one of the warblers, had bolted, and Palemon, who remained, had forgotten what was set down for him, though he obligingly offered to sing "Tom Bowling" instead. But Lady Rasherly thought proper to dispense with the song, and there being nothing else, or better, to do, she directed a movement to the marquee, in order to begin, though somewhat early, on the collation. Alas! even this was a failure. During the time of Gubbins's ducking—the Queen's coronation—and the boxing-match—Hobbinol, that great greedy lout, had been privily in the pavilion, glutting his constitutional voracity on the substantials, and he was now lying insensible and harmless, like a gorged boa constrictor, by the side of the table. Pan too had been missing, and it was thought he was at the Rose and Crown,— but no such luck! He had been having a sly pull at the tent tankards, and from half drunk had got so whole drunk, that he could not hinder his goat from having a butt even at Diana herself, nor from entangling his horns in the table-cloth, by which the catastrophe of the collation was completed!

The rest of the fête consisted of a succession of misfortunes which it would be painful to dwell upon, and cruel to describe minutely. So I will but hint, briefly, how the fragments of the banquet were scrambled for by the Arcadians—how they danced afterwards round the May-pole, not tripping themselves like fairies, but tripping one another—how the Honourable Miss Rasherly, out of idleness, stood fitting the notch of an arrow to the string—and how the shaft went off of itself, and lodged, unluckily, in the calf of one of the caperers. I will leave to the imagination, what suits were torn past mending, or soiled beyond washing—the lamentations of old Jenkins — and the vows of Lady Rasherly and daughters, that there should be no more May-days at Porkington. Suffice it, that night found *all* the Arcadians at the Rose and Crown: and on the morrow, Diana and her Nymphs were laid up with severe colds —Dolly Wiggins was out of place—Hobbinol in a surfeit—Alexis before a magistrate—Palemon at a surgeon's—Billy in the pound—and Pan in the stocks, with the fumes of last night's liquor not yet evaporated from his grey gooseberry eyes.

THE END.

BRADBURY AND EVANS, PRINTERS, WHITEFRIARS.